VOLUME 3

CARMEN LOMAS GARZA TO EDWARD LEAR

FAVORITE CHILDREN'S
AUTHORS AND
ILLUSTRATORS

E. RUSSELL PRIMM III, EDITOR IN CHIEF

TRADITION BOOKS™
EXCELSIOR, MINNESOTA

For Irene Barron Keller, whose love of the English language touched the lives of millions of young readers through her writing and editing

☙

Published by **TRADITION BOOKS**™ and distributed to the school and library market by **THE CHILD'S WORLD**®
P.O. Box 326, Chanhassen, MN 55317-0326
800/599-READ
http://www.childsworld.com

A NOTE TO OUR READERS:

The publication dates listed in each author or illustrator's selected bibliography represent the date of first publication in the United States.

The editors have listed literary awards that were announced prior to June 2005.

Every effort has been made to contact copyright holders of material included in this reference work. If any errors or omissions have occurred, corrections will be made in future editions.

Photographs ©: Candlewick Press: 124; Children's Book Press: 8; E.L. Konigsburg: 136; Farrar, Straus, and Giroux: 68 (Bruce Stotesbury); Harcourt: 16 (Kent Antcliffe), 120; HarperCollins Publishers: 12 (Ellan Young Photography), 32 (Carlo Ontal), 40, 44 (Tom Beckley), 60, 64, 80 (Photocraft, Ltd.), 104 (Philip Gould), 116 (Allan Einhorn); Hulton-Deutsch Collection/CORBIS: 152; Johanna Hurwitz: 76; Kerlan Collection, University of Minnesota: 48, 128 (Karen Hoyle), 148; Patricia Reilly Giff: 24 (Random House/Tim Keating); Penguin Putnam: 56, 88, 108, 112; Scholastic: 20, 36, 52, 96, 140, 144; Simon & Schuster: 28, 72; Suzy Kline: 132; Trina Schart Hyman: 84 (Jean K. Aull).

An Editorial Directions book

LIBRARY OF CONGRESS CATALOGING-IN-PUBLICATION DATA

Favorite children's authors and illustrators / E. Russell Primm, III, editor-in-chief.
    p. cm.
Summary: Provides biographical information about authors and illustrators of books for children and young adults, arranged in dictionary form. Includes bibliographical references and index.
  ISBN 1-59187-018-6 (v. 1 : lib. bdg. : alk. paper)—ISBN 1-59187-019-4 (v. 2 : lib. bdg. : alk. paper)—ISBN 1-59187-020-8 (v. 3 : lib. bdg. : alk. paper)—ISBN 1-59187-021-6 (v. 4 : lib. bdg. : alk. paper)—ISBN 1-59187-022-4 (v. 5 : lib. bdg. : alk. paper)—ISBN 1-59187-023-2 (v. 6 : lib. bdg. : alk. paper) 1. Children's literature—Bio-bibliography—Dictionaries—Juvenile literature. 2. Illustrators—Biography—Dictionaries—Juvenile literature. [1. Authors. 2. Illustrators.]
I. Primm, E. Russell, 1958–
 PN1009.A1 F38 2002
  809'.89282'03—dc21   2002007129

Second printing

TABLE OF CONTENTS

MAJOR CHILDREN'S AUTHOR AND ILLUSTRATOR LITERARY AWARDS

THE AMERICAN BOOK AWARDS
Awarded from 1980 to 1983 in place of the National Book Award to give national recognition to achievement in several categories of children's literature

THE BOSTON GLOBE-HORN BOOK AWARD
Established in 1967 by Horn Book *magazine and the* Boston Globe *newspaper to honor the year's best fiction, poetry, nonfiction, and picture books for children*

THE CALDECOTT MEDAL
Established in 1938 and presented by the Association for Library Service to Children division of the American Library Association to illustrators for the most distinguished picture book for children from the preceding year

THE CARNEGIE MEDAL
Established in 1936 and presented by the British Library Association for an outstanding book for children written in English

THE CARTER G. WOODSON BOOK AWARDS
Established in 1974 and presented by the National Council for the Social Studies for the most distinguished social science books appropriate for young readers that depict ethnicity in the United States

THE CORETTA SCOTT KING AWARDS
Established in 1970 in connection with the American Library Association to honor African-American authors and illustrators whose books are deemed outstanding, educational, and inspirational

THE HANS CHRISTIAN ANDERSEN MEDAL
Established in 1956 by the International Board on Books for Young People to honor an author or illustrator, living at the time of nomination, whose complete works have made a lasting contribution to children's literature

THE KATE GREENAWAY MEDAL
Established by the Youth Libraries Group of the British Library Association in 1956 to honor illustrators of children's books published in the United Kingdom

THE LAURA INGALLS WILDER AWARD
Established by the Association for Library Service to Children division of the American Library Association in 1954 to honor an author or illustrator whose books, published in the United States, have made a substantial and lasting contribution to children's literature

THE MICHAEL L. PRINTZ AWARD
Established by the Young Adult Library Services division of the American Library Association in 2000 to honor literary excellence in young adult literature (fiction, nonfiction, poetry, or anthology)

THE NATIONAL BOOK AWARD
Established in 1950 to give national recognition to achievement in fiction, nonfiction, poetry, and young people's literature

THE NEWBERY MEDAL
Established in 1922 and presented by the Association for Library Service to Children division of the American Library Association for the most distinguished contribution to children's literature in the preceding year

THE ORBIS PICTUS AWARD FOR OUTSTANDING NONFICTION
Established in 1990 by the National Council of Teachers of English to honor an outstanding informational book published in the preceding year

THE PURA BELPRÉ AWARD
Established in 1996 and cosponsored by the Association for Library Service to Children division of the American Library Association and the National Association to Promote Library Services to the Spanish Speaking to recognize a writer and illustrator of Latino or Latina background whose works affirm and celebrate the Latino experience

THE SCOTT O'DELL AWARD
Established in 1982 and presented by the O'Dell Award Committee to an American author who writes an outstanding tale of historical fiction for children or young adults that takes place in the New World

Carmen Lomas Garza

Born: 1948

Carmen Lomas Garza grew up in Kingsville, Texas, not far from the Mexican border. As a child, she was fortunate to have many relatives living in the area. Aunts, uncles, and cousins were often around the house. They chatted, cooked, ate, and played with Carmen and her brothers and sisters. The relatives told wonderful stories about their Indian, Texan, Mexican, and Spanish ancestors. They told Carmen stories about her grandparents and great-grandparents.

Carmen Lomas Garza was born in 1948. Her mother was a self-taught artist. She often painted small pictures for *lotería* cards. They were like bingo cards but with tiny pictures instead of numbers.

GARZA MADE A HUGE CUTOUT OF HER GRANDFATHER WATERING CORN. IT IS FIVE FEET TALL AND EIGHT FEET WIDE!

Carmen's mother would paint the little pictures with ink and watercolor while Carmen watched in wonder. Carmen thought what her mother did was magic. Even then, she thought she might like to be a painter one day.

Carmen started saving the notebook paper she used at school. The back of the paper was blank and perfect for drawing. She spent hours and hours drawing on the backs of the sheets. She drew all kinds of things—hands and feet, people sleeping, pets, pictures in magazines. She took her first art classes in grade school. By the time she was thirteen, she knew for sure that she wanted to be an artist.

"I always wanted to do artwork in color because I remember in color. I remember the clothing in color, the lighting, the walls—you know, just everything in color."

In high school, Carmen took more art classes. She loved them. Her teacher noticed how hard Carmen worked and helped her get a college scholarship. She began studying art at Texas A & I University (now Texas A&M University) in Kingsville right after finishing high school.

Garza always liked to learn from other artists. She often visited other Mexican-American artists to see what they were doing. One time she was visiting some other artists and saw a book on Mexican folk art

A 1991 EXHIBIT OF GARZA'S WORK IN AUSTIN, TEXAS,
DREW MORE THAN ONE THOUSAND VISITORS ON THE FIRST DAY!

MAGIC WINDOWS
Ventanas mágicas

CARMEN LOMAS GARZA

A Selected Bibliography of Garza's Work

Magic Windows/Ventanas mágicas (1999)

Making Magic Windows: Creating Papel Picado/Cut-Paper Art with Carmen Lomas Garza (1999)

In My Family/En mi familia (1996)

Family Pictures/Cuadros de familia (1990)

Garza's Major Literary Awards

2000 Carter G. Woodson Honor Book
2000 Pura Belpré Award for Illustration
  Magic Windows/Ventanas mágicas

1998 Pura Belpré Honor Book for Illustration
  In My Family/En mi familia

1996 Pura Belpré Honor Book for Illustration
  Family Pictures/Cuadros de familia

that explanined how to do cut-paper art called *papel picado*.

Garza gave paper cutting a try and loved it. She started making cutouts of all kinds of designs and images. In time, her cutouts became more and more complex. Some cutouts were pictures from her childhood. They showed her mother making tortillas, family members making paper flowers, and her grandfather trimming a cactus. Garza's book *Magic Windows/Ventanas mágicas* has

"When I was growing up, I was very shy and I didn't speak very much. I didn't learn to speak out until I was in college. My artwork helped me do that."

some of her cutouts, along with English and Spanish explanations. In *Making Magic Windows: Creating Papel Picado/Cut-Paper Art with Carmen Lomas Garza,* Garza explains how to make tissue-paper cutouts called *banderitas.* Garza likes to teach her nieces and nephews this ancient art because she believes this helps connect them to their ancestors.

Garza's paintings also show her memories of daily life in Kingsville. Her book *In My Family/En mi familia* has paintings of a wedding day, a local dance, and people just sitting on the front porch. Another book, *Family Pictures/Cuadros de familia* shows everyday scenes from her childhood. Her brightly colored pictures show how friends and family have always been important in her life.

❧

WHERE TO FIND OUT MORE ABOUT CARMEN LOMAS GARZA

BOOKS

Rockman, Connie C., ed. *Eighth Book of Junior Authors and Illustrators.*
New York: H. W. Wilson Company, 2000.

WEB SITE

CARMEN LOMAS GARZA'S WEB SITE
http://www.carmenlomasgarza.com
To read a biographical sketch of Carmen Lomas Garza, information about
her books, and answers to frequently asked questions

IT TAKES GARZA SEVERAL YEARS TO FINISH PAINTING EACH BOOK. SHE USUALLY
NEEDS FROM THREE TO NINE MONTHS FOR EACH PAINTING!

Jean Craighead George

Born: July 2, 1919

It is sometimes hard for readers to name their favorite book by Jean Craighead George because there are so many. For more than fifty years, George has been writing stories for children. She and her books have won many awards. One book, *My Side of the Mountain,* was even made into a movie.

Jean Craighead George was born on July 2, 1919, in Washington, D.C. Her father was an etymologist. He studied bugs. Jean's brothers, mother, and other relatives also studied nature.

Jean's family loved the outdoors and the plants and animals that lived there. They often went camping in the woods. Jean learned about the plants she could eat and the habits of wild

GEORGE HAS HAD OVER 173 PETS IN HER HOME—BUT NOT AT ONE TIME! MOST OF THEM HAVE BEEN WILD ANIMALS THAT STAY FOR AWHILE AND THEN RETURN TO THE WILD.

animals. She learned skills to survive in the woods.

As Jean grew older, she continued to be interested in nature. But since the third grade, she also loved to write. So after she graduated from Pennsylvania State University with a degree in science and literature, she became a reporter and wrote for many newspapers and magazines.

After marrying and having three children, George began bringing animals home for the family. Tarantulas, a raccoon, owls, robins, and many other

> "It's fascinating how many questions books inspire. Reading puts the brain to work."

A Selected Bibliography of George's Work

Firestorm (2003)
Cliffhanger (2002)
Autumn Moon (2001)
How to Talk to Your Cat (2000)
Frightful's Mountain (1999)
Elephant Walk (1998)
Dipper of Copper Creek (1996)
There's an Owl in the Shower (1995)
The First Thanksgiving (1993)
On the Far Side of the Mountain (1990)
Shark beneath the Reef (1989)
Water Sky (1987)
One Day in the Prairie (1986)
The Talking Earth (1983)
The Wounded Wolf (1978)
Julie of the Wolves (1972)
The Summer of the Falcon (1962)
My Side of the Mountain (1959)

George's Major Literary Awards

1973 Newbery Medal
  Julie of the Wolves

1960 Newbery Honor Book
  My Side of the Mountain

kinds of birds were just some of the animals in their home. Soon, these animals became characters in George's writing.

George's children learned to enjoy nature the same way their mother had as a child. The family often went camping and hiking. These experiences in nature with her family gave George more ideas for her stories. Later, her children went into careers related to science and nature. George's visits with them continue to give her ideas and experiences for her books.

> *"I go to these wonderful places, get to know the people, the animals, the landscape and weather, then come home to Chappaqua, New York, and write my books."*

George was inspired to write the book *Julie of the Wolves* when visiting Barrow, Alaska, with her son Luke. Another visit there provided her with the information and experiences she used to write *Water Sky.* George visited another son in California to gather information for the book *There's an Owl in the Shower.*

Jean Craighead George writes about animals, plants, deserts, forests, and tundra. In her writing, she also teaches her readers about respect for the environment. They learn how people's actions can harm animals and their habitats. George's writing provides children with vivid and absorbing stories. It also provides children with important

GEORGE TRAINED A FALCON WHEN SHE WAS THIRTEEN YEARS OLD. HER BROTHERS WERE TWO OF THE FIRST FALCONERS IN THE UNITED STATES.

knowledge about their world. This knowledge helps them understand how their actions affect the environment and the world around them.

Jean Craighead George lives in Chappaqua, New York. She continues to write about the wonders of nature for young people.

❧

WHERE TO FIND OUT MORE ABOUT JEAN CRAIGHEAD GEORGE

BOOKS
Cary, Alice. *Jean Craighead George.*
Santa Barbara, Calif.: Learning Works, 1996.

Gallo, Don, ed. *Speaking for Ourselves: More Autobiographical Sketches by Notable Authors of Books for Young Adults.* Urbana, Ill.: National Council of Teachers of English, 1997.

George, Jean Craighead. *Journey Inward.*
New York: Dutton, 1982.

WEB SITES
EDUCATIONAL PAPERBACK ASSOCIATION
http://edupaperback.org/showauth.cfm?authid=29
To read an autobiographical sketch by Jean Craighead George
and a list of her books and awards

JEAN CRAIGHEAD GEORGE'S OWN WEB PAGE
http://www.jeancraigheadgeorge.com/
For an autobiographical sketch by Jean Craighead George, photos,
video and audio clips, a booklist, and some tips from the author on writing

---

THE BOOK *WATER SKY* INCLUDES A POLAR BEAR ATTACK. THIS REALLY HAPPENED WHEN GEORGE WAS IN AN INUIT WHALING CAMP IN NORTHERN ALASKA.

Gail Gibbons

Born: August 1, 1944

Gail Gibbons writes and illustrates her own books. She paints with bright, bold, beautiful colors and writes with simple, colorful words. Since 1975, Gibbons has written and illustrated more than 100 books for children from preschool to fifth grade. Mostly nonfiction, her books are filled with interesting facts and creative ideas.

Gail Gibbons was born on August 1, 1944, in Oak Park, Illinois. She was a curious child and became interested in drawing at an early age. A kindergarten teacher recognized Gail's talent and convinced her parents to pay for art lessons.

After graduating from high school, she studied graphic design at

GAIL GIBBONS PUT TOGETHER HER FIRST BOOK WHEN
SHE WAS FOUR YEARS OLD. SHE USED YARN TO BIND THE PAGES TOGETHER.

the University of Illinois, where she met Glenn Gibbons. They married in 1966. The next year she graduated with a degree in fine arts and began working as a graphic artist for WCIA, a local television station in Champaign, Illinois.

In 1970, Gibbons and her husband moved to New York City, where she did artwork for a children's television program on NBC called *Take a Giant Step.* Inspired by children on the show, Gibbons decided to try her hand at writing and illustrating her own stories. It took her five years to accomplish her goal.

"The type of books I write are nonfiction books. This is because I love researching so much. I get to ask lots of questions, just like when I was a kid. I also get to travel and meet lots of interesting people."

In 1972, Gibbons's husband died tragically in an accident. Gibbons began working on NBC's nightly news program. She continued to write and illustrate on the side. In 1975, she published her first book, *Willy and His Wheel Wagon,* which deals with math.

A year later, Gibbons married Kent Ancliffe, a builder, and became stepmother to his two children. They built a home in Corinth, Vermont, where the family now lives. Gibbons spends most of the year at their quaint Vermont farmhouse, writing and illustrating books and

---

IN 1982, GIBBONS EARNED A CERTIFICATE OF APPRECIATION FROM THE U.S. POSTMASTER GENERAL FOR *THE POST OFFICE BOOK: MAIL AND HOW IT MOVES.*

A Selected Bibliography of Gibbons's Work

Mummies, Pyramids, and Pharaohs: A Book about Ancient Egypt (2003)

The Berries Book (2002)

Giant Pandas (2002)

Behold—The Unicorns! (2001)

Ducks! (2001)

Bats (1999)

Marshes & Swamps (1998)

Soaring with the Wind: The Bald Eagle (1998)

Click! A Book about Cameras and Taking Pictures (1997)

Cats (1996)

Christmas on an Island (1994)

Nature's Green Umbrella: Tropical Rain Forests (1994)

Spiders (1993)

Surrounded by Sea: Life on a New England Fishing Island (1991)

Weather Words and What They Mean (1990)

Monarch Butterfly (1989)

Trains (1987)

From Path to Highway: The Story of the Boston Post Road (1986)

Check It Out! The Book about Libraries (1985)

The Milk Makers (1985)

The Seasons of Arnold's Apple Tree (1984)

Cars and How They Go (Illustrations only, 1983)

The Post Office Book: Mail and How It Moves (1982)

The Missing Maple Syrup Sap Mystery; or, How Maple Syrup Is Made (1979)

Willy and His Wheel Wagon (1975)

helping her husband run their maple syrup business.

Ever curious about the world around her, Gibbons writes about what she sees. Often, she explores what is at hand. She has written about the maple syrup business (*The Missing Maple Syrup Sap Mystery; or, How Maple Syrup Is Made*) and their second home on an island in Maine (*Surrounded by Sea: Life on a New England Fishing Island*). Frequent visits to a nearby dairy farm led her to write *The Milk Makers*. And visits to bald eagle nesting sites prompted her to write *Soaring with the Wind: The Bald Eagle*.

Sometimes, her research has taken her to distant places. Once she visited the Florida Everglades to gather information for her book called *Marshes & Swamps*. Another time she toured the islands of Saba and Dominica to do research for the book *Nature's Green Umbrella: Tropical Rain Forests*.

> *"To me, putting a nonfiction book together is like watching the pieces of a puzzle finally fitting together."*

Over the years, Gibbons's books have won many awards. Perhaps the award she cherishes most is the one she receives each time a child reads one of her books and answers the questions Gibbons asked herself before beginning to write: Who lives there? How does that work? Why does that happen? What can I do to have fun?

WHERE TO FIND OUT MORE ABOUT GAIL GIBBONS

BOOKS

Collier, Laurie, and Joyce Nakamura, eds. *Major Authors and Illustrators for Children and Young Adults.* Detroit: Gale Research, 1993.

Kovacs, Deborah, and James Preller. *Meet the Authors and Illustrators: 60 Creators of Favorite Children's Books Talk about Their Work.* Vol. 2. New York: Scholastic, 1993.

WEB SITES

EDUCATIONAL PAPERBACK ASSOCIATION
http://edupaperback.org/showauth.cfm?authid=240
To read a biographical sketch of and a booklist for Gail Gibbons

GAIL GIBBONS: AMERICA'S LEADING NONFICTION AUTHOR
http://www.gailgibbons.com/
To read an autobiographical sketch by Gail Gibbons and a booklist

———

GIBBONS AND HER HUSBAND HAVE A LITTLE FARMHOUSE ON AN ISLAND OFF THE COAST OF MAINE. GIBBONS'S BOOK *CHRISTMAS ON AN ISLAND* IS SET THERE.

James Cross Giblin

Born: July 8, 1933

He has written a book about windows and a book about milk. He has written books about dinosaur bones and human diseases. And the list goes on. James Cross Giblin writes nonfiction books for children. He has written books on a wide range of topics and people.

He has been working as a writer for more than forty-five years. His best-known books include *Chimney Sweeps: Yesterday and Today*, *The Truth about Santa Claus*, *Walls: Defenses throughout History*, and *The Amazing Life of Benjamin Franklin*.

James Cross Giblin was born on July 8, 1933, in

GIBLIN HAS WRITTEN A BOOK CALLED *WRITING BOOKS FOR YOUNG PEOPLE*. THIS BOOK HELPS ADULTS WRITE CHILDREN'S BOOKS.

The Amazing Life of BENJAMIN FRANKLIN

by James Cross Giblin • illustrated by Michael Dooling

Cleveland, Ohio. He grew up in a small town near Cleveland.

As a young boy, James was very shy. He enjoyed reading books and drawing. He read the comic strips in the newspaper and drew his own comic strips. He would draw the pictures, and then his mother would print the words on the strips. He filled many sketchbooks with his comic strips and other drawings.

James also enjoyed going

A Selected Bibliography of Giblin's Work

The Amazing Life of Benjamin Franklin (2000)

The Century That Was: Reflections on the Last One Hundred Years (2000)

The Mystery of the Mammoth Bones: And How It Was Solved (1999)

Charles A. Lindbergh: A Human Hero (1997)

The Dwarf, the Giant, and the Unicorn: A Tale of King Arthur (1996)

When Plague Strikes: The Black Death, Smallpox, AIDS (1995)

Thomas Jefferson: A Picture Book Biography (1994)

Be Seated: A Book about Chairs (1993)

Edith Wilson: The Woman Who Ran the United States (1992)

George Washington: A Picture Book Biography (1992)

The Truth about Unicorns (1991)

The Riddle of the Rosetta Stone: Key to Ancient Egypt (1990)

Let There Be Light: A Book about Windows (1988)

From Hand to Mouth, or, How We Invented Knives, Forks, Spoons, Chopsticks, and the Table Manners to Go with Them (1987)

Milk: The Fight for Purity (1986)

The Truth about Santa Claus (1985)

Walls: Defenses throughout History (1984)

Fireworks, Picnics, and Flags (1983)

Chimney Sweeps: Yesterday and Today (1982)

The Skyscraper Book (1981)

The Scarecrow Book (1980)

Giblin's Major Literary Awards

2001 Orbis Pictus Honor Book
The Amazing Life of Benjamin Franklin

1998 Orbis Pictus Honor Book
Charles A. Lindbergh: A Human Hero

1986 *Boston Globe–Horn Book* Nonfiction Honor Book
The Truth about Santa Claus

1983 American Book Award
Chimney Sweeps: Yesterday and Today

to the movies. He was especially interested in spy flims and movies about World War II (1939–1945).

> "I love research. . . . I enjoy making things clear for readers."

When James Giblin was in junior high school, he began working on the school newspaper. He was not sure he wanted to work on the paper, but his teacher encouraged him to get involved. James discovered that he loved coming up with ideas for stories and pictures for the paper.

In high school, James got involved in school plays. Though he was still very shy, he found that he could reveal his feelings when he was onstage.

Giblin's interest in drama continued in college. He starred in many theater productions as a college student. He even won a contest to appear on a radio drama with a professional actress. Then his interest

> "I try to write books that I would have enjoyed reading when I was the age of my readers."

shifted to directing and writing plays. His first play was written and performed in 1954. In 1955, Giblin earned a master's degree in fine arts from Columbia University.

By 1959, Giblin needed to find a career that was more stable than theater. He took a job as an editor for a publishing company. The new posi-

---

GIBLIN ENJOYED READING THE COMIC STRIP *BLONDIE* WHEN HE WAS GROWING UP.

tion gave him the chance to read and edit books written by other authors. He worked in publishing for more than twenty years before he began writing his own books.

Giblin's first book, *The Scarecrow Book,* was published in 1980. Since that time, he has written more than twenty nonfiction books for young people. Many people like Giblin's books because he is able to write about complex things in a way that is easy to understand.

James Cross Giblin has won many awards for his nonfiction books. He lives in New York City, where he continues to write books for young people.

❧

WHERE TO FIND OUT MORE ABOUT JAMES CROSS GIBLIN

BOOKS

Holtze, Sally Holmes, ed. *Sixth Book of Junior Authors & Illustrators.*
New York: H. W. Wilson Company, 1989.

Something about the Author. Autobiography Series. Vol. 12.
Detroit: Gale Research, 1991.

WEB SITE

UNIVERSITY OF SOUTHERN MISSISSIPPI DE GRUMMOND COLLECTION
http://www.lib.usm.edu/~degrum/findaids/giblin.htm
To read a biographical sketch of and a booklist for James Cross Giblin

———

JAMES CROSS GIBLIN HAS WRITTEN ARTICLES AND STORIES
FOR *COBBLESTONE, HIGHLIGHTS FOR CHILDREN,* AND *CRICKET.*

Patricia Reilly Giff

Born: April 26, 1935

s a young girl, Patricia Reilly Giff dreamed of being a writer. Before becoming a writer, she worked as a teacher and reading consultant for many years. She eventually achieved her dream of writing books for children and young people. She has written dozens of books, including the Kids of the Polk Street School series, the Polka Dot, Private Eye series, and the Ballet Slippers series.

Patricia Reilly Giff was born on April 26, 1935, in Brooklyn, New York. When she was growing up, she almost always had a book in her hands. Her friends would get

---

GIFF OWNS A CHILDREN'S BOOKSTORE IN FAIRFIELD, CONNECTICUT, CALLED THE DINOSAUR'S PAW.

together and play games in the park. Patricia would sit under a tree and read. She also loved to sit with her father and mother and have them read to her.

Patricia often borrowed books from the library. Over the years, she read all the books for children and young people that were in the library. She almost ran out of books to read. But the librarian found books for her from the adult section.

When she finished high school, Giff attended Marymount College in New York. She knew she wanted to be a writer, so she decided to study English. She changed her mind after she read books by famous writers. She did not think she was talented enough to be a writer. She studied history instead.

> *"I spent most of my childhood with a book in my hands. I read before the sun was up, then hunched over the breakfast table with my book in my lap. After school, I'd sit in the kitchen leaning against the warm radiator dreaming over a story."*

After Giff finished college, she became a teacher in the New York City public schools. She got her first teaching job in 1956.

Giff was married in 1959. By the time she was forty years old, she had three children and was a reading teacher in a public school.

GIFF HAS THREE CATS NAMED J.R. FIDDLE, BONNIE, AND JAKE.

A Selected Bibliography of Giff's Work

Pictures of Hollis Woods (2002)
All the Way Home (2001)
Nory Ryan's Song (2000)
Adiós, Anna (1998)
A Glass Slipper for Rosie (1997)
Lily's Crossing (1997)
Dance with Rosie (1996)
Ronald Morgan Goes to Camp (1995)
Ronald Morgan Goes to Bat (1988)
Watch Out, Ronald Morgan! (1985)
The Almost Awful Play (1984)
The Gift of the Pirate Queen (1982)
Have You Seen Hyacinth Macaw? (1981)
The Winter Worm Business (1981)
Today Was a Terrible Day (1980)
The Girl Who Knew It All (1979)
Fourth-Grade Celebrity (1979)

Giff's Major Literary Awards

2003 Newbery Honor Book
  Pictures of Hollis Woods

1998 Newbery Honor Book
1997 *Boston Globe–Horn Book* Fiction Honor Book
  Lily's Crossing

She realized that she had not done any writing.

Since Giff still wanted to be a writer, she decided to start working on a book. "I dragged myself out of bed in the early morning darkness to spend an hour or two at my typewriter before I had to leave for school," Giff notes. It took her several years to finish her first children's book. The book, *Fourth-Grade Celebrity,* was published in 1979. Giff then decided that she would follow her dream of becoming a writer.

> *"Anyone who laughs and cries, anyone who feels, can write. It's only talking on paper . . . talking about things that matter to us."*

Most of Giff's books are written for students in the middle grades. She writes novels and has created several book series. Her books are known for their humor and familiar situations.

Patricia Reilly Giff lives in Connecticut with her husband. This productive author continues to write books for children and young people.

❧

WHERE TO FIND OUT MORE ABOUT PATRICIA REILLY GIFF

BOOKS

Holtze, Sally Holmes, ed. *Fifth Book of Junior Authors & Illustrators.* New York: H. W. Wilson Company, 1983.

Kovacs, Deborah, and James Preller. *Meet the Authors and Illustrators: 60 Creators of Favorite Children's Books Talk about Their Work.* Vol. 2. New York: Scholastic, 1993.

WEB SITES

EDUCATIONAL PAPERBACK ASSOCIATION
http://edupaperback.org/showauth.cfm?authid=30
To read an autobiographical sketch by and a booklist for Patricia Reilly Giff

RANDOM HOUSE: AUTHORS/ILLUSTRATORS
http://www.randomhouse.com/author/results.pperl?authorid=10018
To read a biographical sketch of Patricia Reilly Giff

———

SOME OF GIFF'S FAVORITE CHILDHOOD BOOKS WERE *LITTLE WOMEN,* *THE SECRET GARDEN,* THE BLACK STALLION SERIES, AND THE NANCY DREW SERIES.

Paul Goble

Born: September 27, 1933

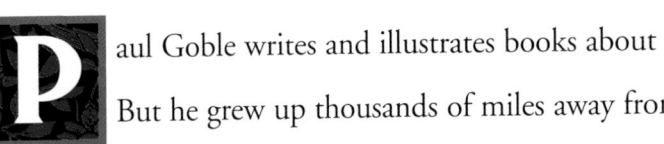

Paul Goble writes and illustrates books about Native American life. But he grew up thousands of miles away from North America.

Paul Goble was born on September 27, 1933, in Surrey, England. As a child, he was fascinated by the lives of American Indians. As Paul grew

older, he longed to know more about their spirituality, stories, and way of life.

Paul Goble studied art at the Central School of Arts and Crafts in London. After he graduated, he stayed in London to work, teaching art and designing furniture.

In 1959, Goble had a chance to visit the United States. Back in England in 1969, he published his first book for children. *Red Hawk's Account of Custer's Last Battle* told the story of a battle between Native Americans

IN 1959, PAUL GOBLE BECAME A MEMBER OF THE YAKIMA AND THE SIOUX TRIBES. HIS INDIAN NAME IS LITTLE THUNDER.

and the U.S. Army from the Native-American point of view.

In 1977, Goble moved to the United States. He was thrilled to have the chance to live, work, and talk with Native Americans. In 1984, he became a U.S. citizen. After living for a while in Nebraska, he settled in South Dakota.

Goble's books are mainly about Native Americans of the plains. He writes and illustrates stories about the Lakota, the

"From early childhood I always wanted to know more [about Native Americans], and to see the country and wildlife with which their lives and beliefs were so closely interwoven."

THE GIRL WHO LOVED WILD HORSES
by PAUL GOBLE

A Selected Bibliography of Goble's Work

Mystic Horse (2002)

Storm Maker's Tipi (2001)

Iktomi Loses His Eyes: A Plains Indian Story (1999)

Iktomi and the Coyote: A Plains Indian Story (1998)

Adopted by the Eagles: A Plains Indians Story of Friendship and Treachery (1994)

Crow Chief: A Plains Indian Story (1992)

Love Flute: Story and Illustrations (1992)

I Sing for the Animals (1991)

Dream Wolf (1990)

Her Seven Brothers (1988)

Iktomi and the Boulder: A Plains Indian Story (1988)

Death of the Iron Horse (1987)

The Great Race of the Birds and Animals (1985)

The Legend of the White Buffalo Woman (1984)

Star Boy (1983)

The Gift of the Sacred Dog: Story and Illustrations (1980)

The Girl Who Loved Wild Horses (1978)

Red Hawk's Account of Custer's Last Battle: The Battle of the Little Bighorn, 25 June 1876 (1969)

Goble's Major Literary Awards

1979 Caldecott Medal
   The Girl Who Loved Wild Horses

Cheyenne, and the Blackfoot. Goble researches stories that have been told and retold for generations. Then he writes them for children and adds brilliant illustrations.

"I feel that I have seen and learned many wonderful things from Indian people which most people would never have the opportunity to experience. I simply wanted to express and to share these things which I love so much."

Goble's pictures often show Native Americans doing everyday tasks or joining in celebrations. They pick berries, make clothing, and gather for dances. Some pictures show beautiful scenes from nature. These pictures often have dozens of small animals or plants in them. At times, Goble paints using bold patterns and silhouettes. Sometimes he uses rich colors and sometimes only earth tones.

Many of Goble's stories are amusing, but they teach serious lessons. They teach children not to be greedy, sneaky, lazy, or dishonest. Other stories show the importance of respecting people, animals, and the environment. Often his characters are animals that can speak or that understand humans.

One of Goble's favorite characters is Iktomi. Iktomi uses tricks to try to get his way. At times, the character appears as a spider. In the Iktomi stories, the trickster is often outsmarted by some other character,

GOBLE'S BOOKS HAVE BEEN CHOSEN FOR THE
LIBRARY OF CONGRESS CHILDREN'S BOOK OF THE YEAR AWARD.

and his plans backfire. The Iktomi stories are most enjoyable when told by a storyteller. The storyteller often asks the listeners questions, trying to lead them deeper into the story.

Although he is himself not an American Indian, Paul Goble has won the respect of many Native Americans. Some of his books have even been used in schools on Lakota reservations to help educate children about their culture.

❧

WHERE TO FIND OUT MORE ABOUT PAUL GOBLE

BOOKS

Kovacs, Deborah, and James Preller. *Meet the Authors and Illustrators: 60 Creators of Favorite Children's Books Talk about Their Work.* Vol. 2. New York: Scholastic, 1993.

McElmeel, Sharron L. *100 Most Popular Picture Book Authors and Illustrators: Biographical Sketches and Bibliographies.* Englewood, Colo.: Libraries Unlimited, 2000.

WEB SITE

UNIVERSITY OF NEBRASKA: PAUL GOBLE
http://monet.unk.edu/mona/exhibit/artists/goble/gobleexh.html
To read a biographical sketch of Paul Goble

———

GOBLE RESEARCHES THE CLOTHING OF NATIVE AMERICAN TRIBES SO HE CAN SHOW IT ACCURATELY IN HIS PAINTINGS.

Virginia Hamilton

Born: March 12, 1936
Died: February 19, 2002

Virginia Hamilton learned the art of storytelling as a young girl from listening to her grandfather, aunts, uncles, and parents. She used her love of storytelling to become an award-winning children's author. Her most popular books include *The House of Dies Drear; Jahdu; The People Could Fly: American Black Folktales;* and *M. C. Higgins, the Great.*

Virginia Hamilton was born on March 12, 1936, in Yellow Springs, Ohio. Her family has lived in Ohio since the 1850s. Virginia's grandfather Levi Perry was a slave in Virginia. He escaped along the Underground Railroad and made it to Ohio. The story of his escape from slavery was often told in Virginia's family. "I

VIRGINIA HAMILTON WAS GIVEN THE NAME VIRGINIA AS A WAY TO
REMEMBER THE STATE WHERE HER GRANDFATHER HAD ESCAPED FROM SLAVERY.

grew up within the warmth of loving aunts and uncles, all reluctant farmers, but great storytellers," Hamilton noted.

Virginia loved school and did well at her studies. She began writing stories as a young girl and read as many books as she could. Virginia was very active in school. She participated in public speaking, sang at public events, and was captain of the girls' basketball team. As a high-school student, she wrote a play that was performed at the school.

Hamilton received a scholarship to study writing at Antioch College. She studied there for three years before transferring to Ohio

"There is no clear way to explain how it is that I never cease having new ideas for books nor the desire to work so intensely at writing them. But as raising a family and keeping up a working farm with my father was my mother's focus and heart, so writing is mine."

State University. She went on to study at a school in New York where she met a young poet named Arnold Adoff. They married in 1960.

Hamilton took many jobs to earn money while she tried to get her writing published. She worked as an accountant, a receptionist, and a singer in a nightclub. Finally, a friend in the publishing business suggested that she expand a short story she had written into a children's book. This story later became her first book, *Zeely*, which was published in 1967. Soon after the book was published, Hamilton and her husband

HAMILTON WAS A BIG FAN OF FROGS—SHE COLLECTED STATUES OF FROGS AND STUFFED FROGS AND WAS EVEN FAMOUS FOR TELLING "FROG JOKES."

A Selected Bibliography of Hamilton's Work

The Girl Who Spun Gold (2000)

Second Cousins (1998)

Her Stories: African American Folktales, Fairy Tales, and True Tales (1995)

Many Thousand Gone: African Americans form Slavery to Freedom (1993)

Cousins (1990)

The Dark Way: Stories From the Spirit World (1990)

The Bells of Christmas (1989)

Anthony Burns: The Defeat and Triumph of a Fugitive Slave (1988)

In the Beginning: Creation Stories from around the World (1988)

Junius over Far (1985)

The People Could Fly: American Black Folktales (1985)

A Little Love (1984)

The Magical Adventures of Pretty Pearl (1983)

Sweet Whispers, Brother Rush (1982)

Justice and Her Brothers (1978)

M. C. Higgins, the Great (1974)

The Planet of Junior Brown (1972)

W.E.B. Du Bois: A Biography (1972)

Zeely (1967)

Hamilton's Major Literary Awards

Virginia Hamilton is one of the most-honored authors of children's books. Due to space constraints, only her major literary awards dating back to 1990 are listed below. For a complete list, please visit Hamilton's Web site at *http://www.virginiahamilton.com/pages/awards.htm*

1996 Coretta Scott King Author Award
   Her Stories: African American Folktales, Fairy Tales, and True Tales

1995 Laura Ingalls Wilder Award

1994 Carter G. Woodson Outstanding Merit Book
   Many Thousand Gone: African Americans from Slavery to Freedom

1992 Hans Christian Andersen Medal for Authors

1990 Coretta Scott King Author Honor Book
   The Bells of Christmas

moved back to Ohio to live near her family.

In her books, Hamilton used African-American characters and emphasized many elements of black history in the United States. Her memories and the experiences she had as a young child are an important part of her books. Because she had such a strong connection to her family, most of her books include a strong sense of family.

Along with writing picture books for children and novels for young adults, Hamilton wrote biographies of famous African-Americans for a young audience. She also edited collections of folktales. Hamilton lived with her husband on her family's land in southern Ohio until her death on February 19, 2002.

> *"My greatest pleasure is sitting down and weaving a tale out of the mystery of my past and present. I'm only thankful that children like my stories as well, my own children included."*

WHERE TO FIND OUT MORE ABOUT VIRGINIA HAMILTON

BOOKS

McElmeel, Sharron L. *100 Most Popular Children's Authors and Illustrators.* Englewood, Colo.: Libraries Unlimited, 1999.

Mikkelsen, Nina. *Virginia Hamilton.* New York: Twayne, 1994.

Wheeler, Jill C. *Virginia Hamilton.* Minneapolis: Abdo & Daughters, 1997.

WEB SITES

DESCRIPTIVE WRITING WITH VIRGINIA HAMILTON
http://teacher.scholastic.com/writewit/diary/
Learn step-by-step how to write descriptive prose

VIRGINIA HAMILTON: WELCOME TO MY WORLD
http://www.virginiahamilton.com/
For an autobiographical account by Virginia Hamilton, book information, and a photo gallery

A TRIP HAMILTON AND HER HUSBAND TOOK TO SPAIN AND NORTH AFRICA GREATLY INFLUENCED HER WRITING, ESPECIALLY *ZEELY.*

Joyce Hansen

Born: October 18, 1942

For years, Joyce Hansen worked as a teacher in the New York City public schools. When she began her career as a writer, she discovered how much she had learned from her students. Years of working with young people gave her insight into the ways of children. "All of my books were inspired by having the opportunity to meet so many young people in my teaching career," Hansen says. "I write realistic fiction about people and places that I know."

Joyce Hansen was born on October 18, 1942, in New York City. Both her mother and her father helped shape Joyce's desire to become a writer. Her mother, Lilian, passed on to Joyce a love for books and reading. Her father, Austin, taught her the art of

---

HANSEN TAUGHT IN PUBLIC SCHOOLS FOR TWENTY-TWO YEARS.

storytelling. He liked to delight Joyce and his other children with stories of his boyhood in the West Indies and his days as a young man in Harlem in the 1920s.

Hansen graduated from Pace University in 1972. She later earned a master's degree from New York University. In 1973, Hansen began teaching in the New York City public schools. She taught children with reading disabilities.

As a teacher, Hansen became convinced of the importance of stories in shaping young lives. "All children need

> *"I write about what I know and what moves me deeply."*

A Selected Bibliography of Hansen's Work

One True Friend (2001)

Bury Me Not in a Land of Slaves: African-Americans in the Time of Reconstruction (2000)

The Heart Calls Home (1999)

Breaking Ground, Breaking Silence: The Story of New York's African Burial Ground (1998)

Women of Hope: African Americans Who Made a Difference (1998)

I Thought My Soul Would Rise and Fly: The Diary of Patsy, a Freed Girl (1997)

The Captive (1994)

Between Two Fires: Black Soldiers in the Civil War (1993)

Out from This Place (1988)

Which Way Freedom? (1986)

Yellow Bird and Me (1986)

Home Boy (1982)

The Gift-Giver (1980)

Hansen's Major Literary Awards

1999 Carter G. Woodson Honor Book
  Women of Hope: African Americans Who Made a Difference

1999 Coretta Scott King Author Honor Book
  Breaking Ground, Breaking Silence: The Story of New York's African Burial Ground

1998 Coretta Scott King Author Honor Book
  I Thought My Soul Would Rise and Fly: The Diary of Patsy, a Freed Girl

1995 Coretta Scott King Author Honor Book
  The Captive

1987 Coretta Scott King Author Honor Book
  Which Way Freedom?

sound, solid literature that relates to their own experiences and interests," she says.

As a writer, Hansen has tried to provide a realistic portrait of the lives of African-American children. Some of her books take place in inner-city neighborhoods today. Others are set in the past and are based on historic events.

Hansen's first novel is set in a New York City neighborhood like the one in which she grew up. The novel is called *The Gift-Giver*, and it was published in 1980. It tells the story of a fifth grader named Doris and her friendship with a shy classmate named Amir. In writing *The Gift-Giver*, Hansen drew on memories of her own childhood in New York.

> *"We must use our words to help our children acquire a richness of soul and spirit, so that perhaps one fine day we will learn to live with ourselves and one another in peace and harmony."*

Hansen wrote three more novels set in New York City. Then, for her next book, she tried a different approach. She wrote about African-Americans in the American South during and after the Civil War (1861–1865).

Before she could write about the past, Hansen had to do research to learn about everyday life during the Civil War. "I was writing about

---

HANSEN GRADUATED FROM COLLEGE WHEN SHE WAS THIRTY YEARS OLD AND PUBLISHED HER FIRST BOOK WHEN SHE WAS THIRTY-EIGHT.

a place and a time of which I had no direct knowledge," she explains. "I had to research my story very carefully because I wanted to be certain that my historical background was correct." *Which Way Freedom?* was named a Coretta Scott King Honor Book in 1987.

In 1994, Hansen published *The Captive,* which tells the story of a West African boy named Kofi who is sold into slavery in the United States in the late 1700s. *The Captive* was also named a Coretta Scott King Honor Book.

Today, Joyce Hansen lives with her husband in South Carolina. She works full-time on her writing.

～

WHERE TO FIND OUT MORE ABOUT JOYCE HANSEN

BOOKS

Collier, Laurie, and Joyce Nakamura, eds. *Major Authors and Illustrators for Children and Young Adults.* Detroit: Gale Research, 1993.

Rockman, Connie C., ed. *Eighth Book of Junior Authors and Illustrators.* New York: H. W. Wilson Company, 2000.

WEB SITE

SCHOLASTIC AUTHORS ONLINE
http://www2.scholastic.com/teachers/authorsandbooks/authorstudies/ authorhome.jhtml?authorID=44&collateralID=5178&displayName=Biography
For an autobiographical sketch by Joyce Hansen, a booklist, and an interview transcript

———

ONE OF HANSEN'S BOOKS, *BREAKING GROUND, BREAKING SILENCE: THE STORY OF NEW YORK'S BURIAL GROUND,* TELLS THE STORY OF AN AFRICAN-AMERICAN BURIAL GROUND IN NEW YORK CITY THAT DATES BACK TO COLONIAL TIMES.

James Haskins

Born: September 19, 1941

James Haskins grew up in Alabama. When he was a young boy, African-Americans were not treated well. They did not have the same rights as white people. When Haskins decided to become a writer, he remembered the hardships of his childhood. He is best known for his nonfiction books for children and young people. His most popular books include *The Picture Life of Malcolm X, Street Gangs: Yesterday and Today, The Story of Stevie Wonder,* and *Black Dance in America: A History through Its People.*

James Haskins was born on September 19, 1941, in Demopolis, Alabama. The town where he grew up was a segregated community.

THE **1984** FILM *THE COTTON CLUB* WAS BASED
ON ONE OF HASKINS'S ADULT NOVELS.

Black people were not allowed to do the same things as white people. There were many places where black people were not allowed to go.

James's family was poor, but he had a happy family life. Storytelling was a big part of his childhood. "My Aunt Cindy was the greatest storyteller who ever lived," Haskins notes. Her stories inspired Haskins to write about things that he experienced.

As a young boy, James loved to read. It was difficult for him to get books because African-Americans were not allowed into the public library. His mother

> *"I knew exactly the kind of books I wanted to do—books about current events and books about important black people so that students could understand the larger world around them through books written at a level they could understand."*

eventually got him an encyclopedia from the supermarket, buying one volume at a time.

James attended a segregated elementary school. Only black children attended the school. The school did not have many books for students to read. Even though the school did not have new books or modern equipment, James had great respect for his teachers.

As a teenager, James moved to Boston, Massachusetts, with his mother. He did well in high school but decided to return to Alabama

WHEN HASKINS WROTE ABOUT THE MUSICIAN STEVIE WONDER, HE WAS ABLE TO MEET WONDER IN LOS ANGELES!

A Selected Bibliography of Haskins's Work

Toni Morrison: Telling a Tale Untold (2002)

Champion: The Story of Muhammad Ali (2001)

Carter G. Woodson: The Man Who Put "Black" in American History (2000)

Bayard Rustin: Behind the Scenes of the Civil Rights Movement (1997)

The Harlem Renaissance (1996)

The March on Washington (1993)

Thurgood Marshall: A Life for Justice (1992)

Outward Dreams: Black Inventors and Their Inventions (1991)

Black Dance in America: A History through Its People (1990)

Black Music in America: A History through Its People (1987)

Lena Horne (1983)

Andrew Young, Man with a Mission (1979)

James Van DerZee: The Picture-Takin' Man (1979)

Barbara Jordan (1977)

The Story of Stevie Wonder (1976)

The Picture Life of Malcolm X (1975)

Street Gangs: Yesterday and Today (1974)

A Piece of the Power: Four Black Mayors (1972)

Haskins's Major Literary Awards

2001 Carter G. Woodson Honor Book
  Carter G. Woodson: The Man Who Put "Black" in American History

1998 Coretta Scott King Author Honor Book
  Bayard Rustin: Behind the Scenes of the Civil Rights Movement

1997 Carter G. Woodson Book Award
  The Harlem Renaissance

1994 Carter G. Woodson Book Award
  The March on Washington

1993 Carter G. Woodson Outstanding Merit Book
  Thurgood Marshall: A Life for Justice

1992 Carter G. Woodson Outstanding Merit Book
  Outward Dreams: Black Inventors and their Inventions

1991 Coretta Scott King Author Honor Book
1988 Carter G. Woodson Book Award
  Black Music in America: A History through Its People

1984 Coretta Scott King Author Honor Book
  Lena Horne

1980 Carter G. Woodson Outstanding Merit Book
1980 Coretta Scott King Author Honor Book
  James Van DerZee: The Picture-Takin' Man

1980 Coretta Scott King Author Honor Book
  Andrew Young, Man with a Mission

1978 Coretta Scott King Author Honor Book
  Barbara Jordan

1977 Coretta Scott King Author Award
  The Story of Stevie Wonder

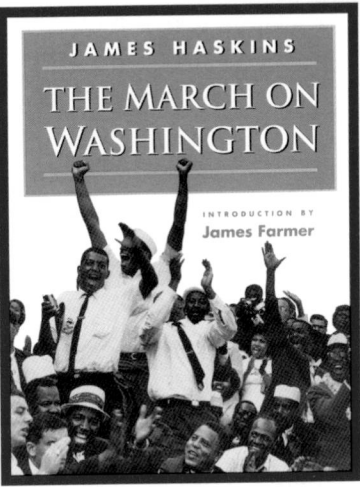

after graduation. Haskins went to college in Alabama for a short time. He was also involved in the civil rights movement in the South. He eventually attended universities in Washington, D.C., and New Mexico.

After finishing college, Haskins went to work for a stock brokerage firm. He didn't find the work very fulfulling, so he got a job as a special education teacher. The people he worked with encouraged him to keep a journal about his experiences as a teacher. His journal writing resulted in his first book, *Diary of a Harlem Schoolteacher.* Publishers then asked Haskins to write more books for children. Since then, he has written more than 100 nonfiction books for children and young people.

> *"Since my first major reading was the encyclopedia, this is probably another reason why I prefer nonfiction."*

James Haskins has also taught writing at several colleges and universities. He lives in Florida and teaches at the University of Florida. He continues to write books for children and young people.

❧

WHERE TO FIND OUT MORE ABOUT JAMES HASKINS

BOOKS

Berger, Laura Standley, ed. *Twentieth-Century Young Adult Writers.* 1st ed. Detroit: St. James Press, 1994.

Something about the Author. Autobiography Series. Vol. 3. Detroit: Gale Research, 1978.

Sutherland, Zena. *Children & Books.* 9th ed. New York: Addison Wesley Longman, 1997.

WEB SITES

CHILDRENSLIT.COM
http://www.childrenslit.com/f_haskins.html
To read a biographical sketch of James Haskins and descriptions of some of his books

———

HASKINS WAS GUEST CURATOR FOR A SMITHSONIAN INSTITUTION TRAVELING EXHIBITION CALLED *THE JAZZ AGE IN PARIS,* WHICH OPENED IN WASHINGTON, D.C. IN 1997.

Kevin Henkes

Born: November 26, 1960

Sometimes adults do know just how you feel. In the books of Kevin Henkes, the children are not perfect. They have the problems that many kids face. They sometimes feel lonely or too messy or a little awkward. The bespectacled Henkes seems to know just how painful childhood can be. He also captures the humor of growing up and the sense of intrigue in a child's day-to-day life. Ever since Henkes was a child he wanted to be an artist, which made him a little different from most of his classmates.

Kevin Henkes was born on November 26, 1960, in Racine, Wisconsin, the son of Barney and

---

KEVIN HENKES'S *A WEEKEND WITH WENDELL* WAS NAMED A CHILDREN'S CHOICE BOOK BY THE CHILDREN'S BOOK COUNCIL AND THE INTERNATIONAL READING ASSOCIATION.

Beatrice Henkes. He has three brothers and a sister.

As a child, Kevin could often be found drawing, coloring, and painting. He loved his art classes, and he says that everyone thought of him as an artist, even at a young age. He seems never to have doubted it himself.

When Henkes was just nineteen years old, he flew to New York City with his drawings and a map of the city. The map must have led him to the

> "I'm a very lucky person. I've known for a very long time that I wanted to be an artist and a writer—and that's exactly what I do for a living."

A Selected Bibliography of Henkes's Work

Kitten's First Full Moon (2004)

Olive's Ocean (2003)

Wemberly's Ice Cream Star (2003)

Owen's Marshmallow Chick (2002)

Sheila Rae's Peppermint Stick (2001)

Wemberly Worried (2000)

The Birthday Room (1999)

Oh! (Text only, 1999)

Circle Dogs (Text only, 1998)

Sun & Spoon (1998)

Lilly's Purple Plastic Purse (1996)

The Biggest Boy (Text only, 1995)

Protecting Marie (1995)

Owen (1993)

Words of Stone (1992)

Chrysanthemum (1991)

Julius, the Baby of the World (1990)

Shhhh (1989)

Chester's Way (1988)

The Zebra Wall (1988)

Sheila Rae, the Brave (1987)

Two under Par (1987)

Grandpa & Bo (1986)

A Weekend with Wendell (1986)

Bailey Goes Camping (1985)

Return to Sender (1984)

Margaret & Taylor (1983)

Clean Enough (1982)

All Alone (1981)

Henkes's Major Literary Awards

2005 Caldecott Medal
   Kitten's First Full Moon

2004 Newbery Honor Book
   Olive's Ocean

1994 *Boston Globe–Horn Book* Picture Book Honor Book
1994 Caldecott Honor Book
   Owen

right place, for he landed a contract that led to his first book, which he called *All Alone*. Henkes says he will never forget that day in New York when his career began. At the time, he was a freshman in college, studying at the University of Wisconsin at Madison.

> *"When I was younger, I wondered about authors and illustrators. What did they look like? Where did they live? Did they have families? How old were they? And now I am one myself. Sometimes it's hard to believe."*

After college, he married Laura Dronzek. Henkes has been a writer and illustrator ever since.

A young character—who is often a mouse—is usually the focus of one of Henkes's picture books. His characters have distinctive personalities with real problems. His readers find out how Sophie learned to like Wendell, what Chester's way is, how Julius becomes the baby of the world, and why Wemberly worried.

In Henkes's picture books, the child's world is seen through the child's eyes. Through his words, illustrations, and humor, Henkes has shown that although he has grown into an adult, he can still live in the world of a child. Henkes has also written several young adult novels.

Kevin Henkes lives with his wife and children in Madison, Wisconsin. He works on his books almost every day.

IN 2000, HENKES WAS INVITED TO WRITE THE INTRODUCTION TO STORIES ABOUT BABAR, THE WORLD'S MOST FAMOUS ELEPHANT. IT APPEARS IN *BONJOUR, BABAR! THE SIX UNABRIDGED CLASSICS BY THE CREATOR OF BABAR.*

&

WHERE TO FIND OUT MORE
ABOUT KEVIN HENKES

BOOKS

Holtz, Sally Holmes, ed. *Sixth Book of Junior Authors & Illustrators.*
New York: H. W. Wilson Company, 1989.

Silvey, Anita, ed. *Children's Books and Their Creators.*
Boston: Houghton Mifflin, 1995.

WEB SITES

EDUCATIONAL PAPERBACK ASSOCIATION
http://edupaperback.org/showauth.cfm?authid=31
To read an autobiographical sketch by and a booklist for Kevin Henkes

HARPERCHILDRENS.COM
http://www.harperchildrens.com/catalog/author_xml.asp?authorid=16903
To read a brief biographical sketch of Kevin Henkes, and to find
links to sites with information on each of his books

KEVIN HENKES'S WEB SITE
http://www.kevinhenkes.com
To read an interview with Henkes, to find out more about
Henkes's characters, and to download book-related games.

———

KEVIN HENKES WORKED WITH HIS WIFE, LAURA DRONZEK, ON ONE BOOK.
OH! WAS WRITTEN BY HENKES AND ILLUSTRATED BY DRONZEK.

Marguerite Henry

Born: April 13, 1902
Died: November 26, 1997

Marguerite Henry wrote many books about dogs, birds, and even mules. But her most famous book is about a horse named Misty and the two orphaned children who are drawn to her. *Misty of Chincoteague* was published in 1947 and has since sold more than a million copies. It won many awards and honors and is considered a classic of children's literature. Although Henry wrote about animals in the great outdoors and lived much of her life on a farm, she was born and raised in a city.

Marguerite Henry was born on April 13, 1902, in Milwaukee, Wisconsin. Marguerite's father owned a publishing company. When she

ONE OF MARGUERITE HENRY'S BOOKS, *KING OF THE WIND*, WON THE NEWBERY MEDAL. *KING OF THE WIND* TELLS THE STORY OF AN ARABIAN STALLION IN THE 1700S WHO STARTED THE LINE OF TODAY'S THOROUGHBRED RACEHORSES.

was a little girl, Marguerite liked to go to her father's business on Saturdays and watch books being printed. One day when she was ten, her father let Marguerite look at a set of proofs—the pages that show how a book will look once it is printed. She decided on the spot that she would become a writer.

Marguerite's father bought her a writing table and writing supplies, and Marguerite began working on her dream. When she was eleven, she submitted an essay about autumn to a popular women's magazine. The magazine printed the essay, and Marguerite's writing career had begun.

Henry attended Milwaukee State Teachers College. There, she continued writing, and she also acted in plays. After she graduated, she married a salesman named Sidney Crocker Henry.

The newlywed couple bought a farm in Wayne, Illinois, and settled there. Marguerite Henry began writing professionally. She sold articles and stories to magazines such as *Reader's Digest,* the *Saturday Evening Post,* and *Forum.*

Henry published her first book for children in 1940. It was called

> *"Stepping softly in the sand, the burro sneaked behind the prospector and playfully butted him up from his crouching position. The old man spun around, his face lighting with joy. 'Brighty!' he shouted happily."*
> —*from* **Brighty of the Grand Canyon**

HENRY'S BOOKS HAVE BEEN TRANSLATED INTO SEVERAL LANGUAGES, INCLUDING URDU, ARABIE, AND AFRIKAANS.

A Selected Bibliography of Henry's Work

Brown Sunshine of Sawdust Valley (1996)

Misty's Twilight (1992)

San Domingo, the Medicine Hat Stallion (1972)

Mustang, Wild Spirit of the West (1966)

Stormy, Misty's Foal (1963)

Five O'Clock Charlie (1962)

Black Gold (1957)

Brighty of the Grand Canyon (1953)

Album of Horses (1951)

Born to Trot (1950)

Sea Star: Orphan of Chincoteague (1949)

King of the Wind (1948)

Misty of Chincoteague (1947)

Justin Morgan Had a Horse (1945)

Auno and Tauno: A Story of Finland (1940)

Henry's Major Literary Awards

1949 Newbery Medal
  King of the Wind

1948 Newbery Honor Book
  Misty of Chincoteague

1946 Newbery Honor Book
  Justin Morgan Had a Horse

Auno and Tauno: A Story of Finland. In 1945, her book *Justin Morgan Had a Horse* was published. It told the story of the founding of the Morgan breed of horses in Vermont. Henry worked with illustrator Wesley Dennis on the book. Henry and Dennis worked well together and eventually, they worked together on some twenty books.

Their second book was their most successful. It was *Misty of Chincoteague.* The book is set on Chincoteague Island, off the coasts of Virginia and Maryland. Henry based the story on a real horse that she found when she visited the island. She even brought the real Misty home to live on her

Illinois farm with her for several years. *Misty of Chincoteague* won many major prizes for children's literature. Its honors include the Lewis Carroll Shelf Award, one of publishing's most important prizes.

> *"The ponies were exhausted and their coats were heavy with water, but they were free, free, free!"*
> —from Misty of Chincoteague

Henry continued to write stories about Misty for nearly fifty years. In all, she wrote more than fifty books. Marguerite Henry died on November 26, 1977.

❧

WHERE TO FIND OUT MORE ABOUT MARGUERITE HENRY

BOOKS

Collins, David. *Write a Book for Me: The Story of Marguerite Henry.*
Greensboro, N.C.: Morgan Reynolds, 1999.

Henry, Marguerite. *A Pictorial Life Story of Misty.*
Chicago: Rand McNally, 1976.

WEB SITE

GREENVILLE PUBLIC LIBRARY: JUVENILE
BOOKS AUTHOR OF THE MONTH
http://www.yourlibrary.ws/childrens_webpage/j-author42001.html
To read a detailed biographical sketch of Marguerite Henry

A LIFE-SIZE STATUE OF THE REAL-LIFE MISTY STANDS ON CHINCOTEAGUE ISLAND.

Karen Hesse

Born: August 29, 1952

Many of Karen Hesse's novels take place in the distant past and in faraway places. Before she writes her novels, Hesse does careful research to help her understand everyday life in other times and places. "I love research," she says. "I love dipping into another time and place."

Karen Hesse was born on August 29, 1952, in Baltimore, Maryland. As a child, she was often ill. She found comfort in reading. Her favorite reading spot was a hideaway in the limbs of an apple tree in her backyard. Karen spent hours there reading her favorite stories. She also was a frequent visitor to the Enoch Pratt Free Library near her home.

THE IDEA FOR THE NOVEL *THE MUSIC OF DOLPHINS* CAME
FROM AN INTERVIEW HESSE HEARD ON THE RADIO.

She began reading Dr. Seuss books at the library and formed a fascination with storytelling that has lasted all her life.

By the time Karen was a teenager, she was reading books written for adults. One of those books had an especially strong impact on her. It was John Hersey's *Hiroshima,* which tells the story of the dropping of an atomic bomb on a Japanese city during World War II (1939–1945). Many years later, Hesse wrote her own novel on a similar topic. *Phoenix Rising* is about the horrors of a nuclear disaster.

"I love writing. I can't wait to get to my desk every morning."

A Selected Bibliography of Hesse's Work

Stone Lamp: A Hanukkah Collection (2002)
Witness (2001)
Stowaway (2000)
Come On, Rain (1999)
A Light in the Storm: The Civil War Diary of Amelia Martin (1999)
Just Juice (1998)
Out of the Dust (1997)
The Music of Dolphins (1996)
A Time of Angels (1995)
Phoenix Rising (1994)
Sable (1994)
Lavender (1993)
Lester's Dog (1993)
Poppy's Chair (1993)
Letters from Rifka (1992)
Wish on a Unicorn (1991)

Hesse's Major Literary Awards

1998 Newbery Medal
1998 Scott O'Dell Award
   Out of the Dust

In high school, Karen became interested in acting. She joined an acting group and performed in amateur productions. Later, she studied drama at Towson State College in Maryland for two years. However, she cut her studies short to marry Randy Hesse.

Eventually, Hesse finished college at the University of Maryland. She graduated in 1975 with a degree in English. While attending the university, Hesse began writing and giving readings of her poetry.

After graduation, Hesse worked at a series of jobs. She was a secretary, a librarian, a substitute teacher, and a proofreader—a person who checks for mistakes in books and other printed material. Hesse and her husband settled in Vermont and had two daughters—Kate born in 1979, and Rachel, born in 1982.

"Writing is not easy. I work for long hours and sometimes all that work disappoints me and I throw it out and begin again."

Hesse's first novel, *Wish on a Unicorn*, was published in 1991. The following year, Hesse published *Letters from Rifka.* It tells the story of a young Jewish girl in Russia in the early 1900s. To escape the brutality of war, her family leaves Russia to live in the United States. However, Rifka becomes separated from her family and has to find her own way to the United States.

In 1997, Hesse published *Out of the Dust.* The novel takes place

HESSE WORKED IN THE COLLEGE LIBRARY TO HELP PAY FOR HER EDUCATION.

in Oklahoma during the 1930s. A drought destroyed farms all across the middle of the United States during those years. Rich soil was turned into dust, and the entire middle of the country was called the Dust Bowl. Hesse's novel tells how a father and daughter survive the terrible poverty of the time. Hesse won the 1998 Newbery Medal for *Out of the Dust.*

Karen Hesse sitll lives in Vermont with her family. She continues to write for young people, whom she calls "the most challenging, demanding, and rewarding audiences."

❧

WHERE TO FIND OUT MORE ABOUT KAREN HESSE

BOOKS

Rockman, Connie C., ed. *Eighth Book of Junior Authors and Illustrators.* New York: H. W. Wilson Company, 2000.

Something about the Author. Vol. 74. Detroit: Gale Research, 1993.

WEB SITES

EDUCATIONAL PAPERBACK ASSOCIATION
http://edupaperback.org/showauth.cfm?authid=56
To read an autobiographical sketch by and a booklist for Karen Hesse

SCHOLASTIC AUTHORS ONLINE
http://www2.scholastic.com/teachers/authorsandbooks/authorstudies/
authorhome.jhtml?authorID=45&collateralID=5183&displayName=Biography
For an autobiographical sketch by Karen Hesse, a booklist, and an interview transcript

---

HESSE RISES AT 5 A.M. EACH DAY TO BEGIN WRITING.

Eric Hill

Born: September 7, 1927

Eric Hill discovered by accident that children like to look behind the flaps of books. He was working on an advertising project that had movable flaps, and his young son kept opening the panels to

see what was behind them. Just as children like to open the doors of cupboards to see inside, they also like to open the flaps of Hill's children's books and discover all sorts of funny creatures staring back at them. The book is almost like a toy, and some books even have movable panels so that children can create their own designs and pictures.

ERIC HILL'S STORIES ABOUT SPOT THE DOG WERE MADE INTO A TELEVISION SHOW CALLED *ADVENTURES OF SPOT* BY THE BRITISH BROADCASTING CORPORATION.

Eric Hill was born in London, England, on September 7, 1927. He liked drawing from an early age. After World War II (1939–1945) began in 1939, Eric was taken away from London to avoid German air force planes that pummeled the city with bombs. Like many other children, though, he found life in the countryside dull compared to life in London. Soon he returned to the city.

Eric became fascinated by the fighters and bombers that flew over London. He learned the names of the planes and sketched them on his drawing pad. Later in the war, he got a job as a messenger and a sweeper at an art studio in London. One of the artists introduced him to cartooning, and Eric began to develop the simple lines and childlike style of his drawings.

"I consider myself very fortunate indeed to have created a character which has captured the imagination and enthusiasm of so many children worldwide. They are my family, and Spot belongs to them all."

From 1945 until 1948, Hill served in the Royal Air Force. After leaving the military, he began his career as an illustrator and designer for advertisements.

Hill was married from 1950 until 1972 to Barbara Hobson, and in 1973 to Gillian McCarthy. He has two children, Jane and Christopher.

THE SPOT BOOKS HAVE BEEN TRANSLATED INTO SIXTY-FIVE LANGUAGES. PART OF THE REASON THAT SPOT IS IN SUCH DEMAND IS THAT THE STORIES ARE SIMPLE AND EASY TO UNDERSTAND IN ANY LANGUAGE.

A Selected Bibliography of Hill's Work

Spot's Little Book of Fun at the Beach (2003)

Spot's Little Book of Fun in the Garden (2003)

Spot's Treasure Hunt (2002)

Spot Goes Splash! And Other Stories (2000)

Good Night, Spot (1999)

Spot's Favorite Baby Animals (1997)

Spot's Walk in the Woods (1993)

Spot at Home (1991)

Spot Goes to the Circus (1986)

Spot at Play (1985)

Baby Bear's Bedtime (1984)

My Pets (1983)

Where's Spot? (1980)

It was Christopher's curiosity that sparked Hill's interest in redesigning children's books. And it was for Christopher that Hill began to draw a puppy named Spot. Hill had found that many children's books were unsuitable for small children, so he kept Spot's adventures simple. The reader follows Spot on his first walk, to his first birthday party, and to school. Children can follow Spot through the same adventures that they themselves have. Indeed, the Spot books seem to have filled a void in children's

> *"I love dogs, and it seemed that the easiest thing for me to do was to draw something I loved."*

literature—by telling simple stories that even very young children can grasp. Hill has also been praised for depicting Spot with simple lines, much the way a child would draw.

Since making Spot one of the most famous dogs in literature, Eric Hill has moved to California. There, he continues to write, surrounded by a large collection of metal toys.

❧

WHERE TO FIND OUT MORE ABOUT ERIC HILL

BOOKS

Children's Literature Review. Vol. 13. Detroit: Gale Research, 1987.

Holtze, Sally Holmes, ed. *Sixth Book of Junior Authors & Illustrators.* New York: H. W. Wilson Company, 1989

WEB SITES

THE OFFICIAL SPOT WEB SITE
http://www.funwithspot.com/
To take an interactive tour of Spot's world, including trips to the farm and the beach

PENGUIN PUTNAM
http://www.penguinputnam.com/static/packages/us/yreaders/Spot/bio.htm
To read a biographical sketch of and a booklist for Eric Hill

---

WHERE'S SPOT?, ERIC HILL'S FIRST SPOT BOOK, WOULD PROBABLY HAVE NEVER BEEN PUBLISHED IF A FRIEND HADN'T TAKEN A SAMPLE OF IT TO A BOOK FAIR IN FRANKFURT, GERMANY. HILL HADN'T SERIOUSLY THOUGHT ABOUT PUBLISHING IT.

Tana Hoban

Tana Hoban is fascinated by familiar objects. They are everyday things—a bowl, a spoon, a sunflower. But have you seen them like this before? Her photograph of a bowl brings out its beauty. She turns her camera to the spoon, and its curving body takes on life. Everyday objects that we hardly notice as we handle them are given their own personality in the photographs of Tana Hoban.

Tana Hoban was born in Philadelphia, Pennsylvania. Her family moved to a country house in Lansdale, Pennsylvania, before Tana started school. In the countryside, she slept on a screened porch until the weather turned too cold. She helped her family raise pigeons and

HOBAN'S PHOTOGRAPHS HAVE BEEN EXHIBITED IN THE UNITED STATES AND FRANCE. THEY ARE PART OF THE NEW YORK MUSEUM OF MODERN ART'S COLLECTION.

bees, tend the garden, and feed the chickens.

On weekends, she studied art, and found that she was quite good at it. Tana was so good that she won a scholarship to Moore College of Art. Following graduation, she went to Europe to work on her paintings.

When Hoban returned from Europe, she began a promising career as an illustrator. Her work was featured in magazines and in advertisements. It was during this time that she met a photographer named Edward Gallob.

Gallob not only gave her her first camera, he also became her husband. They had a daughter, Miela.

A Selected Bibliography of Hoban's Work

Cubes, Cones, Cylinders, & Spheres (2000)
I Wonder (1999)
Construction Zone (1997)
Just Look (1996)
Animal, Vegetable, or Mineral? (1995)
What Is That? (1994)
Black on White (1993)
All about Where (1991)
Exactly the Opposite (1990)
Shadows and Reflections (1990)
Panda, Panda (1986)
A Children's Zoo (1985)
Is It Larger? Is It Smaller? (1985)
1, 2, 3 (1985)
Round and Round and Round (1983)
Take Another Look (1981)
Is It Red? Is It Yellow? Is It Blue? (1978)
Where Is It? (1978)
Push, Pull, Empty, Full: A Book of Opposites (1972)
Look Again! (1971)
Shapes and Things (1970)

Hoban's Major Literary Awards

1985 *Boston Globe–Horn Book* Special Citation
   1, 2, 3

> *"My books are about everyday things that are so ordinary that one tends to overlook them. I try to rediscover these things and share them with children."*

Although the couple later divorced—and Hoban would marry John G. Morris—Gallob's gift of the camera changed her future. Hoban had never really studied photography, but she found that she had a good sense of light and an eye for interesting pictures. She especially liked to photograph children. Hoban's photos were featured in magazines and included in exhibitions. But Hoban always dreamed of collecting the photographs and presenting them to children.

Her first book, *Shapes and Things,* did just that. It is an exploration of shapes, a celebration of these simple things. Hoban used black-and-white photographs instead of the traditional color illustrations of most children's books. There are no words. The objects alone parade across the pages. A thing is interesting in itself, Hoban seems to be saying. Children respond well to the book. Even adults sometimes feel as if they are glimpsing the child's world through Hoban's photographs.

> *"I believe certain things happen when the time is right. I also believe that anybody can do anything he or she really wants to."*

TANA HOBAN HAS CONDUCTED CHILDREN'S PHOTOGRAPHY WORKSHOPS IN FRANCE, TAUGHT PHOTOGRAPHY AT THE UNIVERSITY OF PENNSYLVANIA, AND LECTURED AT MANY OTHER SCHOOLS IN THE UNITED STATES.

The title of Hoban's second book, *Look Again!,* seems to sum up her approach perfectly. Shapes catch her interest. Black-and-white photographs remove the distraction of color. Sometimes Hoban focuses on a texture. Her photographs bring out the roughness or smoothness of an object. Wherever she chooses to point her camera, the world becomes a little more fascinating.

Tana Hoban lives in Paris, France. This gifted photographer continues to work on her books for children.

❧

WHERE TO FIND OUT MORE ABOUT TANA HOBAN

BOOKS

Contemporary Authors. Vol. 23. Detroit: Gale Research, 1981.

De Montreville, Doris, and Elizabeth D. Crawford, eds. *Fourth Book of Junior Authors & Illustrators.* New York: H. W. Wilson Company, 1978.

WEB SITES

UNIVERSITY OF SOUTHERN MISSISSIPPI DE GRUMMOND COLLECTION
http://www.lib.usm.edu/%7Edegrum/html/research/findaids/hobantan.htm
To read a biographical sketch of and a booklist for Tana Hoban

---

TANA HOBAN HAS APPLIED HER SKILL WITH STILL PHOTOGRAPHY TO MOVING PICTURES. IN 1967, SHE PRODUCED THE FILM *CATSUP.* SHE LATER PRODUCED THE FILMS *WHERE IS IT?* AND *PANDA, PANDA.*

Syd Hoff

Born: September 4, 1912

Died: May 12, 2004

For a short time in college Syd Hoff wanted to be a serious painter. He was inspired by the old masters and other great painters— Rembrandt, Edouard Manet, Leonardo da Vinci. But there was something a little off about his paintings. No matter how hard he tried to paint

seriously, a comic streak kept showing through. His teachers had their doubts, and so did Hoff, for he liked to draw funny things and was very good at it. Today, he is famous for his newspaper comic strips and for books such as *Danny and the Dinosaur.* It seems that Syd Hoff was a pretty funny kid from the start.

Sydney Hoff was born on September 4, 1912, in New York City. His father, Benjamin, was a salesman. His mother,

SYD HOFF'S *DANNY AND THE DINOSAUR* WAS MADE INTO A FILMSTRIP BY WESTON WOODS STUDIO.

Mary, was very supportive of Syd's early interest in drawing. When he

was only three years old, Syd drew a picture of a subway conductor, with his brass-button uniform and conductor's hat. His mother pegged the picture to a wall with a three-inch nail and proclaimed her son to be an artist.

> *"I was born three years after the date of my birth. The family had gone for a ride in the subway and when we came home I drew a picture of the conductor . . . my mother said, 'Sydney is an artist,' and I've been trying to live up to her words ever since."*

Support for Syd's artistic aspirations came flooding in from other directions, too. When a cartoonist visited his high school, Syd was singled out to join him onstage and draw a cartoon. The cartoonist also proclaimed Syd to be a future artist.

Aside from art class, however, Syd was a miserable student. He dropped out of high school before finishing his last year. Syd still wanted to study art though, so he lied about his age and was accepted to the National Academy of Design in New York City. There he got to know the works of many famous artists and was encouraged by his teachers to take up something else.

At age eighteen, Hoff took that advice. He submitted one of his cartoon drawings to *The New Yorker* magazine, which is famous for publishing witty cartoons. That cartoon started a long relationship

---

CBS BELIEVED THAT SYD HOFF'S HUMOR WOULD WORK WELL ON TELEVISION, AND THEY GAVE HIM HIS OWN TV SERIES CALLED *TALES OF HOFF*.

A Selected Bibliography of Hoff's Work

Danny and the Dinosaur Go to Camp (1996)
Happy Birthday, Danny and the Dinosaur! (1995)
Duncan the Dancing Duck (1994)
Bernard on His Own (1993)
Barney's Horse: Story and Pictures (1987)
The Man Who Loved Animals (1982)
Play Ball with Roger the Dodger (1980)
Arthur Gets What He Spills (1979)
Barkley (1975)
The Horse in Harry's Room (1970)
Irving and Me (1967)
Grizzwold (1963)
Albert the Albatross (1961)
Oliver (1960)
Julius (1959)
Sammy the Seal (1959)
Danny and the Dinosaur (1958)

between Hoff and *The New Yorker,* which continued to publish his work. Then, for ten years starting in 1939, his comic strip about a girl named Tuffy appeared in the newspapers and reached millions of readers.

Hoff married Dora Berman in 1937, and the couple had two daughters, Susan and Bonnie. When one of his daughters was undergoing physical therapy, Hoff sketched pictures of a dinosaur and a young boy to cheer her up. The pictures were published as *Danny and the Dinosaur.*

Hoff had tried once before to write a book for children, but it was not much of a hit. *Danny and the Dinosaur,* on the other hand, launched a new career for him as a successful children's book author. His drawings are simple pen and ink, sometimes watercolors. They depict the lighthearted world of Danny and his friend the dinosaur, who is on holiday for a day from the museum. Syd Hoff never became a serious painter, but he has entertained many children with his drawings and has become famous for being able to make people laugh.

> *"Humor, for some reason, is basically sad. There's some sort of affinity between the sad and the funny that makes it all the funnier."*

❧

WHERE TO FIND OUT MORE ABOUT SYD HOFF

BOOKS

De Montreville, Doris, and Donna Hill, eds. *Third Book of Junior Authors.*
New York: H. W. Wilson Company, 1972.

Something about the Author. Vol. 72.
Detroit: Gale Research, 1993.

WEB SITE

HARPERCHILDRENS.COM
http://www.harperchildrens.com/catalog/author_xml.asp?authorID=12221
To find out more about Syd Hoff and his books

———

SYD HOFF IS MOST FAMOUS AS A CARTOONIST AND ILLUSTRATOR, BUT HE IS ALSO THE AUTHOR OF MYSTERY STORIES THAT HAVE BEEN PUBLISHED IN *ALFRED HITCHCOCK'S MYSTERY MAGAZINE* AND *ELLERY QUEEN'S MYSTERY MAGAZINE.*

Polly Horvath

Born: January 30, 1957

Adults often like Polly Horvath's books as much as young readers do. That's just fine with Horvath. She doesn't believe in calling some books "children's books" and other books "adult books." "When I was a child, my mother used to tell us that anybody can read anything," Horvath says. "I didn't like *Charlotte's Web* as a kid, but I adore it as an adult. This idea of reading within your age slot is bunk. Read what you like."

Polly Horvath was born on January 30, 1957, in Kalamazoo, Michigan. Her father, John, was a teacher. Her mother, Betty, was a writer. When Polly was a girl, her parents encouraged her interest in

---

HORVATH SAYS HER WRITING HAS BEEN INFLUENCED BY THE WORK OF CHARLES DICKENS AND MARK TWAIN.

reading. By the time she was nine, Polly had begun writing her first stories. She continued to write all through her childhood and teen years.

When she turned eighteen, Horvath decided to pursue another talent. She began studying dance. She attended the Martha Graham School of Contemporary Dance in New York and the Canadian College of Dance in Toronto, Ontario. She planned to pursue a career as a dance teacher. In Canada, she met her husband, Arnold Keller, an English professor. Horvath has lived in Canada since 1975.

Horvath continued to write stories and send them to publishers. Although she was

A Selected Bibliography of Horvath's Work
The Canning Season (2002)
Everything on a Waffle (2001)
The Trolls (1999)
When the Circus Came to Town (1996)
The Happy Yellow Car (1994)
No More Cornflakes (1990)
An Occasional Cow (1989)

Horvath's Major Literary Awards
2003 National Book Award
   The Canning Season
2002 Newbery Honor Book
2001 *Boston Globe–Horn Book* Fiction and Poetry Honor Book
   Everything on a Waffle
1999 *Boston Globe–Horn Book* Fiction Honor Book
   The Trolls

> *"It's not the natural disasters you have to fear. It's the ones inside you, waiting to happen."*

sometimes discouraged by rejections, she did not give up.

Finally, in 1989, she published her first book, *An Occasional Cow.* The book is about a ten-year-old girl named Imogene who goes to stay with cousins in Iowa for one summer. The following year, Horvath published her second book, *No More Cornflakes.* In *No More Cornflakes,* a ten-year-old girl named Hortense has to survive big changes in her family, including her mother expecting a baby.

Horvath's next book was set during the hard times of the Great Depression of the 1930s. In *The Happy Yellow Car,* Betty Grunt is shocked when her father comes home with a fancy yellow car, which he bought with money the family had saved for Betty's college education.

Horvath's 1999 book, *The Trolls,* shows her affection for her adopted country, Canada. Aunt Sally from Canada comes to visit her nieces and nephews who live in Ohio. At first, the children don't know what to make of Aunt Sally, but she eventually wins them over.

Horvath's book *Everything on a Waffle* is her first to be set in Canada. Set in a town on the Pacific coast of Canada, the book is about a girl named Primrose Squarp. Although everyone tells Primrose

---

NICKELODEON IS AT WORK ON A PRODUCTION OF *THE TROLLS.*

that her parents have been lost at sea, Primrose refuses to believe it. One of the book's themes is the way people can deal with loss without losing hope.

Polly Horvath lives with her husband and two daughters in Metchosin, British Columbia. She is at work on more novels— one for children and two for adults.

> *"I don't feel I approach a new book. I always feel a new book approaches me. I just sit down and write."*

᠀

WHERE TO FIND OUT MORE ABOUT POLLY HORVATH

WEB SITES

CHILDREN'S AUTHOR INTERVIEW: POLLY HORVATH
http://www.nancymatson.com/authorwriterviews/horvat.htm
To read a brief biography of and interview with Polly Horvath

KIDSREADS.COM
http://www.kidsreads.com/reviews/0374322368.asp
To read a synopsis of Polly Horvath's *Everything on a Waffle*

HORVATH IS ONLY THE SECOND CANADIAN RESIDENT
TO HAVE EARNED A NEWBERY HONOR.

James Howe

Born: August 2, 1946

umor is an important part of James Howe's books. "Humor is the most precious gift I can give to my reader," Howe has said. He has written more than fifty books for children and young people. He has written picture books, novels, and screenplays for movies and television shows. His most popular books include the Bunnicula series, the Sebastian Barth series, and the Pinky and Rex series.

James Howe was born on August 2, 1946, in Oneida, New York. As a young boy, he enjoyed making up stories with his friends. His

BUNNICULA: A RABBIT-TALE OF MYSTERY, THE STORY OF A PET RABBIT THAT IS THOUGHT TO ACT LIKE A VAMPIRE, WAS ADAPTED INTO AN ANIMATED TELEVISION MOVIE THAT AIRED IN **1982.**

family also stimulated his imagination and interest in words and writing. "Words played an important part in my growing up," Howe says. "Not only the written word, but words that flew through the air—jokes, riddles, puns. My family was always playing with words."

James found writing to be fun and entertaining. He wrote and performed in his first play when he was seven years old. Later, he wrote short stories and humor columns for his high school newspaper. He even published his own newspaper that he called the *Gory Gazette*.

When Howe entered college at Boston University, he wanted to become an actor rather than a writer. "As much as I loved writing plays, I loved performing in them even more," Howe notes. He received a fine arts degree in 1968 and worked as a social worker for a short time. He then pursued his acting career and appeared in television commercials. Howe also directed several plays and worked as an agent for other writers.

A few years later Howe went to graduate school and took a play-writing class, which reminded him of his love for writing. Howe's wife,

> *"Most of my stories are humorous, but they almost always have something serious going on in them as well. That's because I can no more separate my serious concerns about the world from my cockeyed way of seeing it than I can keep apart my personal and professional selves."*

IN HIS NONFICTION BOOK *THE HOSPITAL BOOK,* HOWE
DESCRIBES MEDICAL PROCEDURES FROM A CHILD'S POINT OF VIEW.
THIS BOOK HELPS CHILDREN UNDERSTAND WHAT IT IS LIKE TO BE IN A HOSPITAL.

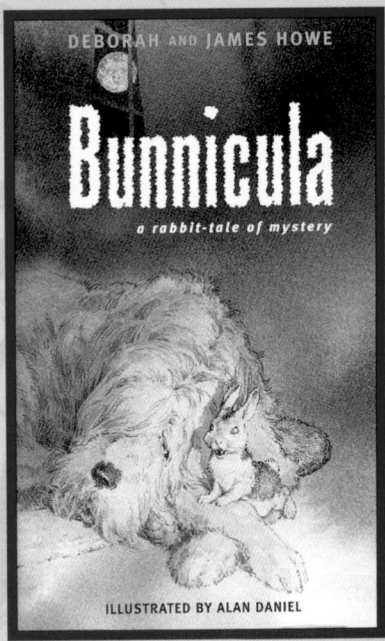

ILLUSTRATED BY ALAN DANIEL

A Selected Bibliography of Howe's Work

Howie Monroe and the Doghouse of Doom (2002)

Invasion of the Mind Swappers from Asteroid 6 (2002)

Horace and Morris Join the Chorus (But What about Dolores?) (2001)

Horace and Morris But Mostly Dolores (1999)

Harold & Chester in Scared Silly: A Halloween Treat (1998)

There's a Dragon in My Sleeping Bag (1994)

Rabbit-Cadabra! (1993)

Return to Howliday Inn (1992)

Harold & Chester in Creepy Crawly Birthday (1991)

Eat Your Poison, Dear (1990)

There's a Monster under My Bed (1990)

Harold & Chester in the Fright before Christmas (1988)

Nighty-Nightmare (1987)

When You Go to Kindergarten (1986)

Howliday Inn (1986)

What Eric Knew: A Sebastian Barth Mystery (1985)

Dew Drop Dead: A Sebastian Barth Mystery (1984)

The Day the Teacher Went Bananas (1984)

The Celery Stalks at Midnight (1983)

The Hospital Book (1981)

Bunnicula: A Rabbit-Tale of Mystery (1979)

Howe's Major Literary Awards

1981 *Boston Globe–Horn Book* Nonfiction Honor Book
   The Hospital Book

Deborah, encouraged him to write a children's book about a rabbit character that he had created several years earlier.

At the same time, Deborah became sick with cancer. As a way to cope with the illness, James and Deborah worked together on this book. Deborah died of cancer in 1978, but the book, *Bunnicula: A Rabbit-Tale of Mystery,* was published in 1979. Howe also published one other book that he cowrote with Deborah. He went on to write many more *Bunnicula* books and other book series for children.

Howe's books are full of humor, but they also include serious issues. He believes that it is important to be open and honest when writing for young people. "It's the writer's privilege and responsibility to give children a world they can enter, recognize, at times be frightened of, but which ultimately, they can master and control," Howe says.

> *"I don't believe I was born to write. But the creative itch has been with me for as long as I can remember. And it has always been strong enough that it demanded to be scratched."*

Howe lives in Hastings-on-Hudson, New York, with his second wife and their daughter. He continues to write both fiction and nonfiction books for children and young people.

∾

WHERE TO FIND OUT MORE ABOUT JAMES HOWE

BOOKS

Holtze, Sally Holmes, ed. *Sixth Book of Junior Authors & Illustrators.* New York: H. W. Wilson Company, 1989.

Howe, James. *Playing with Words.* Katonah, N.Y.: Owen, 1994.

WEB SITE

SCHOLASTIC AUTHORS AND BOOKS
http://www2.scholastic.com/teachers/authorsandbooks/authorstudies/authorhome.jjhtml?authorid =1832&collateralID=10322&displayName=Biography
To read a biography of James Howe and to explore his books

SOME OF HOWE'S WORKS HAVE BEEN TRANSLATED INTO FRENCH, GERMAN, SWEDISH, DANISH, ITALIAN, JAPANESE, SPANISH, AND DUTCH.

Johanna Hurwitz

Born: October 9, 1937

Johanna Hurwitz has written more than fifty books for young readers. Even as a child, books were an important part of her life. Johanna Hurwitz was born in New York City on October 9, 1937. Her father, Nelson, was a journalist and bookseller. Her mother, Tillie, was a library assistant. The walls of the family's New York apartment were lined with books. Johanna herself became interested in books at an early age. She applied for a public library card as soon as she was old enough. Before she was ten, she had decided that she would become a professional writer.

While in high school, Johanna began working at the New York Public Library. She graduated from Queens

---

JOHANNA HURWITZ'S FATHER ONCE RAN A USED BOOKSTORE IN NEW YORK CITY.

College in 1958, and received a master's degree in library science from Columbia University in 1959. After graduation, she began working as a full-time children's librarian. She married Uri Hurwitz in 1962. The couple have two children, Nomi and Benjamin.

Hurwitz began writing stories when she was a girl. However, she did not publish her first book until 1976. It was called *Busybody Nora,* and it was based on her own experiences raising her two children. *Busybody Nora* is the story of a curious seven-year-old, a character inspired by Hurwitz's daughter, Nomi. Nora's little brother, Teddy, is based on Hurwitz's son, Benjamin.

A Selected Bibliography of Hurwitz's Work

Dear Emma (2002)
Oh No, Noah! (2002)
Ethan at Home (2001)
Superduper Teddy (2001)
Pee Wee's Tale (2000)
Aldo Ice Cream (1999)
Aldo Peanut Butter (1999)
The Just Desserts Club (1999)
A Dream Come True (1998)
Ever-Clever Elisa (1997)
Helen Keller: Courage in the Dark (1997)
The Down & Up Fall (1996)
Elisa in the Middle (1995)
A Word to the Wise: And Other Proverbs (1994)
Leonard Bernstein: A Passion for Music (1993)
Roz and Ozzie (1992)
New Neighbors for Nora (1991)
Nora and Mrs. Mind-Your-Own Business (1991)
Astrid Lindgren: Storyteller to the World (1989)
Hurray for Ali Baba Bernstein (1989)
Anne Frank: Life in Hiding (1988)
Class Clown (1987)
Russell Sprouts (1987)
The Adventures of Ali Baba Bernstein (1985)
The Hot & Cold Summer (1985)
The Rabbi's Girls (1982)
Tough-Luck Karen (1982)
Baseball Fever (1981)
Aldo Applesauce (1979)
The Law of Gravity: A Story (1978)
Busybody Nora (1976)

Nora also appears in several other Hurwitz books, including *Nora and Mrs. Mind-Your-Own-Business* and *New Neighbors for Nora*. Teddy is the main character in a book called *Superduper Teddy.* "It seems as if all my fiction has grown out of real experiences," Hurwitz once explained. "It took me many years to realize that my everyday life contained the substance for the books I fantasized I would write."

Her children's love of baseball helped inspire Hurwitz's book *Baseball Fever*. A summer vacation in Vermont inspired *Yellow Blue Jay*. Stories of her mother's childhood were the basis for her book *The Rabbi's Girls*.

Hurwitz has invented several fictional families that make repeat appearances in her books. For example, the Sossi family is featured in *Aldo Ice Cream*. In that book, fourth-grader Aldo Sossi sets out to sample every flavor at the local ice cream parlor. In *Aldo Peanut Butter,* he raises puppies named Peanut and Butter. Aldo's thirteen-year-old sister Karen is the main character in *Tough-Luck Karen.* Another sister is featured in *Hurricane Elaine.*

> *"I write for children because I am especially interested in that period of life. There is an intensity and seriousness about childhood that fascinates me."*

Hurwitz has also written several books about real people. She is the author of four biographies of important historical figures. Her book *Anne Frank: Life in Hiding* tells the story of the now-famous Jewish girl who

WHEN SHE WAS A GIRL, JOHANNA HURWITZ LIVED SO CLOSE TO YANKEE STADIUM IN NEW YORK THAT SHE COULD HEAR BASEBALL FANS CHEERING FROM HER HOUSE.

lived in hiding danger during World War II (1939–1945). *Astrid Lindgren: Storyteller to the World* is about the creator of the Pippi Longstocking books. *Leonard Bernstein: A Passion for Music* introduces young readers to the American conductor and composer. *Helen Keller: Courage in the Dark* is about the famous blind and deaf American author.

> *"If upon completion of my book, the reader is eager to read another (by me or by someone else too), then I know I have been successful."*

Hurwitz lives in Great Neck, New York. She continues to be inspired to write books for children.

&

WHERE TO FIND OUT MORE ABOUT JOHANNA HURWITZ

BOOKS

Kovacs, Deborah, and James Preller. *Meet the Authors and Illustrators: 60 Creators of Favorite Children's Books Talk about Their Work.* Vol. 2. New York: Scholastic, 1993.

Silvey, Anita, ed. *Children's Books and Their Authors.* Boston: Houghton Mifflin, 1995.

WEB SITES

EDUCATIONAL PAPERBACK ASSOCIATION
http://edupaperback.org/showauth2.cfm?authid=135
To read an autobiographical sketch and booklist for Johanna Hurwitz

HARPERCOLLINS CHILDREN'S BOOKS: JOHANNA HURWITZ
http://www.harperchildrens.com/authorintro/index.asp?authid=14706
To read a biography of Johanna Hurwitz, to read about her life in her own words, and to explore her many books

HURWITZ OWNS TWO CATS, SINBAD AND SELENA.

Pat Hutchins

Born: June 18, 1942

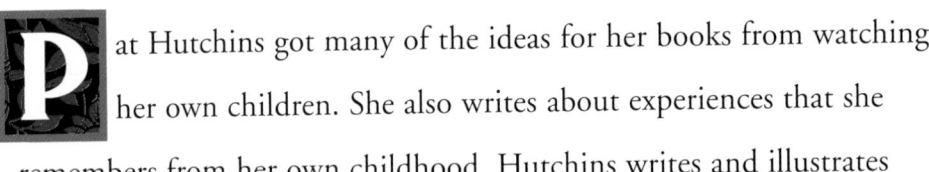

Pat Hutchins got many of the ideas for her books from watching her own children. She also writes about experiences that she remembers from her own childhood. Hutchins writes and illustrates

picture books. Her best-known books include *The Very Worst Monster, The Wind Blew, Where's the Baby?,* and *Tidy Titch.* Hutchins has also written several fiction books for young people, which her husband, Laurence Hutchins, illustrated.

Pat Hutchins was born on June 18, 1942, in Yorkshire, England. She grew up the sixth of seven children. Pat loved to wander around the countryside with her friends. Pat liked to read, draw, and often carried her sketch pad with her.

HUTCHINS WROTE *HAPPY BIRTHDAY, SAM* FOR HER OWN SON SAM.

Pat's mother often took care of injured animals. One of the animals that Pat's mother nursed back to health was a crow. Pat named the crow Sooty. Pat let the crow sit on her shoulder. When she walked in the woods, Sooty went with her!

When she was sixteen years old, Pat received a scholarship to attend a local art school. She studied there for three years. She then went on to study illustration at Leeds College of Art in England.

After college, Hutchins went to London to find a job. She was hired by an advertising agency. She met and married her husband while working at the agency. Just days after they were married, he was transferred to the agency's office in New York City.

Hutchins and her husband lived in a small apartment in New York City. She did not have much to do and decided to spend her time writing and illustrating a children's book.

In 1968, after eighteen months, the couple moved back to London. That year her first son was born and her first book, *Rosie's Walk,* was published. Her second son was born five years later. Since then, Pat Hutchins has written and illustrated more

> *"I feel that ultimately you write to satisfy yourself and hope that your readers will be satisfied with your offering, too."*

TIDY TITCH IS BASED ON HUTCHINS'S SONS, SAM AND MORGAN.

The Doorbell Rang
by Pat Hutchins

A Selected Bibliography of Hutchins's Work

Only One of Me (2003)
We're Going on a Picnic! (2001)
Ten Red Apples (2000)
Tidy Titch (1999)
It's My Birthday! (1998)
Shrinking Mouse (1997)
Clocks and More Clocks (1994)
Little Pink Pig (1994)
My Best Friend (1993)
Where's the Baby? (1988)
The Doorbell Rang (1986)
The Very Worst Monster (1985)
King Henry's Palace (1983)
One-Eyed Jake (1979)
The Best Train Set Ever (1978)
The Wind Blew (1974)
Good Night, Owl! (1972)
Changes, Changes (1971)
Rosie's Walk (1967)

Hutchins's Major Literary Awards

1974 Kate Greenaway Medal
    The Wind Blew

1999 *Boston Globe–Horn Book* Picture Book Honor Book
    Rosie's Walk

than thirty books for children.

Hutchins enjoys writing for children. "I think one can get quite complicated ideas across to small children as long as they are presented in a simple, satisfying way," Hutchins notes. She includes humor in her books and writes about things from the lives of children.

Hutchins lives in a part of London called Hampstead with her husband. She continues to write and illustrate books for children and young people.

"To me, the most important thing about a children's picture book is that it should be logical."

~

Where to Find Out More About Pat Hutchins

Books

Collier, Laurie, and Joyce Nakamura, eds. *Major Authors and Illustrators for Children and Young Adults.* Detroit: Gale Research, 1993.

Kovacs, Deborah, and James Preller. *Meet the Authors and Illustrators: 60 Creators of Favorite Children's Books Talk about Their Work.* Vol. 1. New York: Scholastic, 1991.

Web Sites

Carol Hurst Children's Literature Site
http://www.carolhurst.com/authors/hutchins.html
For a brief biographical sketch of Pat Hutchins and synopses of several of her books

Titch by Pat Hutchins
http://www.titch.net
To read about Hutchins's books, to see photgraphs of the author, and find out answers to questions frequently asked of Hutchins.

As a young child, Hutchins lived in an army training camp. She played in the fields where the soldiers did their training.

Trina Schart Hyman

Born: April 8, 1939
Died: November 19, 2004

If you have ever seen pictures of Saint George battling a dragon to save the English kingdom or beautiful pictures of Sleeping Beauty, you may have seen the work of Trina Schart Hyman. Her illustrations have brought to life more than a hundred children's stories. She has given children images of knights battling evil in a halo of light and of monsters that are truly horrible to look upon.

The creator of these fantastic visions was born in Philadelphia, Pennsylvania, on April 8, 1939, the daughter of Albert Schart, a salesman, and Margaret Doris Schart. Trina Hyman has said that the secret of turning a fictional character into a memorable picture is a fascination with people—their characters, expressions, and

TRINA SCHART HYMAN'S VIVID ILLUSTRATIONS LEND THEMSELVES TO FILM ADAPTATIONS. *DRAGON STEW, TIGHT TIMES,* AND *LITTLE RED RIDING HOOD* HAVE ALL BEEN MADE INTO FILMSTRIPS OR TELEVISION SPECIALS.

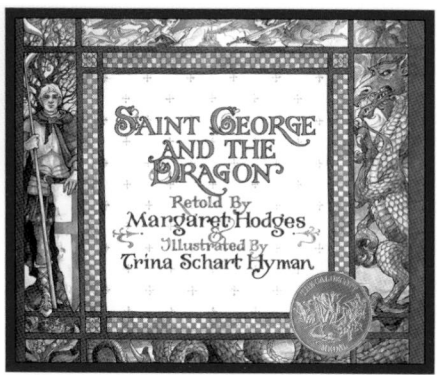

behaviors. She has tried to discover what makes a knight dashing, a maiden beautiful, or a monster frightening. Then she makes it plain to the reader through her drawings and paintings. Her gift for art was enhanced by training at the Philadelphia Museum College of Art and the Boston Museum School of the Arts.

In 1959, she married Harris Hyman. The couple has one daughter, Katrin. In 1960, Hyman was admitted to the Swedish State Art School. She

A Selected Bibliography of Hyman's Work

Little Women, or, Meg, Jo, Beth, and Amy (Illustrations only, 2002)

Children of the Dragon: Selected Tales from Vietnam (Illustrations only, 2001)

The Alphabet Game (2000)

A Child's Calendar (Illustrations only, 1999)

A Smile So Big (Illustrations only, 1998)

Comus (Illustrations only, 1996)

Winter Poems (Illustrations only, 1994)

The Fortune-Tellers (Illustrations only, 1992)

Ghost Eye (Illustrations only, 1992)

Hershel and the Hanukkah Goblins (Illustrations only, 1989)

A Child's Christmas in Wales (Illustrations only, 1985)

Saint George and the Dragon: A Golden Legend (Illustrations only, 1984)

Little Red Riding Hood (1983)

Tight Times (Illustrations only, 1979)

On to Widecombe Fair (Illustrations only, 1978)

King Stork (Illustrations only, 1973)

Dragon Stew (Illustrations only, 1969)

All in Free but Janey (Illustrations only, 1968)

Hyman's Major Literary Awards

2000 Caldecott Honor Book
   A Child's Calendar

1993 *Boston Globe–Horn Book* Picture Book Award
   The Fortune-Tellers

1990 Caldecott Honor Book
   Hershel and the Hanukkah Goblins

1985 Caldecott Medal
   St. George and the Dragon

1984 Caldecott Honor Book
   Little Red Riding Hood

1978 *Boston Globe–Horn Book* Picture Book Honor Book
   On to Widecombe Fair

1976 *Boston Globe–Horn Book* Nonfiction Honor Book
   Will You Sign Here, John Hancock?

1973 *Boston Globe–Horn Book* Picture Book Award
   King Stork

1968 *Boston Globe–Horn Book* Picture Book Honor Book
   All in Free but Janey

> *"One of the nicest things about being an artist is the ability to see things a little differently, . . . more carefully, . . . more imaginatively, than most other people do . . . to see the possibilities in things, to see the magic, . . . to see what it is that makes that thing inherently itself."*

struggled to master Swedish and landed her first job as an illustrator. When she returned to the United States, she was offered an illustrating job by one of her friends who worked at Little, Brown Publishing. It was just the first of many such projects. Her illustrations proved to be popular with authors and readers. She has a knack for capturing a book's atmosphere. Her illustrations give the characters real personalities, no matter how minor their role in the story.

In 1972, Hyman took a job as art director of *Cricket* magazine. Aside from designing covers and laying out the interiors, she came into contact with many writers and illustrators. This brought her many offers to illustrate books. She is perhaps most famous for her illustrations of classic children's tales. She has illustrated stories by the Brothers Grimm, Charles

> *"The focus of my illustrations— largely because of the kinds of stories I choose to illustrate—is almost always on human beings. People—and this includes monsters and other fantastic creatures—are endlessly fascinating to me as subject matter."*

TRINA SCHART HYMAN RECEIVED HER FIRST ILLUSTRATING JOB WHILE STUDYING IN SWEDEN. SHE SAYS THAT IT TOOK HER NEARLY AS LONG TO READ THE BOOK IN SWEDISH AS IT DID TO DO THE ILLUSTRATIONS.

Dickens, Mark Twain, and Hans Christian Andersen. Her depiction of the medieval world, with its knights, castles, monks, village girls, and princes has earned much attention. Her painting captures the finery of a noble's robes and the wretchedness of an old hag. In her work, the world of fantasy and magic seems real and fantastic at the same time. Hyman has a romantic vision, more stunning than reality, and it captures the wonder of the world of the imagination and of times long forgotten. Through Trina Schart Hyman's vision, fantastic stories come to life, giving children images that might well stay with them for a lifetime.

❧

WHERE TO FIND OUT MORE ABOUT TRINA SCHART HYMAN

BOOKS

Hyman, Trina Schart. *Self Portrait: Trina Schart Hyman.*
Reading, Mass.: Addison-Wesley, 1981.

Kovacs, Deborah, and James Preller. *Meet the Authors and Illustrators: 60 Creators of Favorite Children's Books Talk about Their Work.* Vol. 1. New York: Scholastic, 1991.

WEB SITES

UNIVERSITY OF SOUTHERN MISSISSIPPI DE GRUMMOND COLLECTION
http://www.lib.usm.edu/%7Edegrum/html/research/findaids/hyman.htm
To read a biographical sketch and booklist for Trina Schart Hyman

WOMEN CHILDREN'S BOOK ILLUSTRATORS
http://www.ortakales.com/illustrators/Hyman.html
To read a biographical sketch of Trina Schart Hyman, a summary
of her awards, and synopses of some of her books

———

BESIDES PAINTING MEDIEVAL AND FAIRY-TALE CHARACTERS, TRINA SCHART HYMAN
DEPICTS LIFE IN PLACES AS FAR AWAY AS WEST AFRICA AND SOUTHEAST ASIA.

Rachel Isadora

Born: 1953

As a young girl, dancing was an important part of Rachel Isadora's life. She spent many years training to be a dancer. Many of her books for children are about dancing and the arts. Isadora has written and illustrated more than forty books for children. Her best-known books include *Ben's Trumpet, My Ballet Diary, Isadora Dances,* and *Sophie Skates.*

Rachel Isadora was born in 1953, in New York City. She began taking dance lessons when she was a toddler after she wandered into her older sister's dance class. She took many different dance lessons and became a very good dancer. When Rachel was eleven years old,

---

ISADORA IS BEST KNOWN FOR HER BOOK *BEN'S TRUMPET,*
WHICH WAS A **1980** CALDECOTT HONOR BOOK.

she performed with a professional ballet company. She also received

a scholarship to attend a

ballet school.

Rachel was very shy as a young girl. She would not practice her dances when people could see her. She would observe in her dance class. Then she would rehearse by herself until she learned the

> *"Work like this is a dancer's fantasy. Because ballet is so demanding, dancers' stage careers are short. They can only dream of going on and on forever. With art, I can go on and on, and for me it's the only work that compares in intensity and joy."*

dance moves. She let people watch her dance only after she had

learned the steps.

Rachel also felt a great deal of pressure as a dancer. Then she

discovered that she liked to draw. She used her drawing as a way to

release the pressure. "To escape it, I drew—so that became my fantasy

world," she noted. "I could express my thoughts in it, I could even

express my anger. I couldn't do that as a dancer." She did not show

her drawings to anyone. She did not even show the drawings to

her parents.

When Rachel was seventeen years old, she was offered a chance to

dance with a professional ballet company in New York. But she felt

---

ISADORA AND HER HUSBAND, JAMES TURNER, HAVE ONE DAUGHTER, GILLIAN.

A Selected Bibliography of Isadora's Work

On Your Toes: A Ballet ABC (2003)
Bring On That Beat (2002)
Nick Plays Baseball (2001)
123 Pop! (2000)
Sophie Skates (1999)
Isadora Dances (1998)
My Ballet Diary (1995)
At the Crossroads (1994)
Prayers, Praises, and Thanksgivings (Illustrations only, 1992)
Swan Lake (1991)
The Little Match Girl (Illustrations only, 1987)
Opening Night (1984)
A Little Interlude (Illustrations only, 1980)
Ben's Trumpet (1979)
Backstage (1978)
Max (1976)

Isadora's Major Literary Awards

1979 *Boston Globe–Horn Book* Picture Book Honor Book
1980 Caldecott Honor Book
   Ben's Trumpet

too much pressure and did not do it. She did not dance for several years. She then had a chance to dance for a ballet company in Boston. But she injured her foot and was no longer able to dance. She needed to find a way to earn money.

Isadora decided to look for a job as an illustrator. She showed her collection of drawings to publishers in New York. It did not take long for her to find work. She was asked to work on a children's book. The book, *Max,* was published in

> *"I see the way a child sees. So I decided, I'll just draw it the way I see it, and the kids will see it their way."*

1976. She has written and illustrated many other books for children during her career.

Isadora continues to write for children and young people. She lives in New York with her family.

◈

WHERE TO FIND OUT MORE ABOUT RACHEL ISADORA

BOOKS

Holtze, Sally Holmes, ed. *Fifth Book of Junior Authors & Illustrators.*
New York: H. W. Wilson Company, 1983.

WEB SITE

PENGUIN PUTNAM: RACHEL ISADORA
http://us.penguingroup.com/nf/Author/AuthorPage/0,,0_10000016301,00.html
For a brief biographical sketch and photo of Rachel Isadora

———

ISADORA AND HER FIRST HUSBAND, ROBERT MAIORANO, WORKED TOGETHER ON
SEVERAL BOOKS. TWO OF THEM ARE *BACKSTAGE* AND *A LITTLE INTERLUDE.*

Brian Jacques

Born: June 15, 1939

Authors of great children's books sometimes write a story for a specific child or group of children, never imagining or intending that it will be published. This happened with *Alice in Wonderland* and *The Hobbit,* for example. It was also the case with Brian Jacques and his book *Redwall,* the first of what would become an enormously popular series.

Brian Jacques was born in Liverpool, England, on June 15, 1939. Like many people in this port city, Brian's family was originally from County Cork in Ireland. Growing up near the Liverpool docks, Brian imagined himself heading off to sea for many adventures.

Growing up, Brian's imagination was fueled by the adventure books he loved reading. Books such as *Robinson Crusoe, Treasure Island,* and *A Wind in the Willows,* and the adventures of characters such as Sherlock

WHEN BRIAN WAS TEN YEARS OLD, HE WROTE A STORY ABOUT A BIRD THAT CLEANS A CROCODILE'S TEETH, AND HIS TEACHER ACCUSED HIM OF COPYING THE STORY FROM SOMEWHERE ELSE.

Holmes, King Arthur, and Tarzan filled his mind with tales of excitement, and bravery.

Attending St. John's, an inner-city school whose playground was on its roof, Brian Jacques began writing stories at the age of ten. His favorite teacher, Mr. Austin Thomas, introduced Brian to poetry and Greek literature when Brian was fourteen. At St. John's, Brian also met a teacher named Alan Durband, who many years later would have a profound impact on his life.

When Brian finished school at age fifteen, his craving for adventure led him to board a ship and set sail as a merchant seaman, a common occupation for young men in Liverpool.

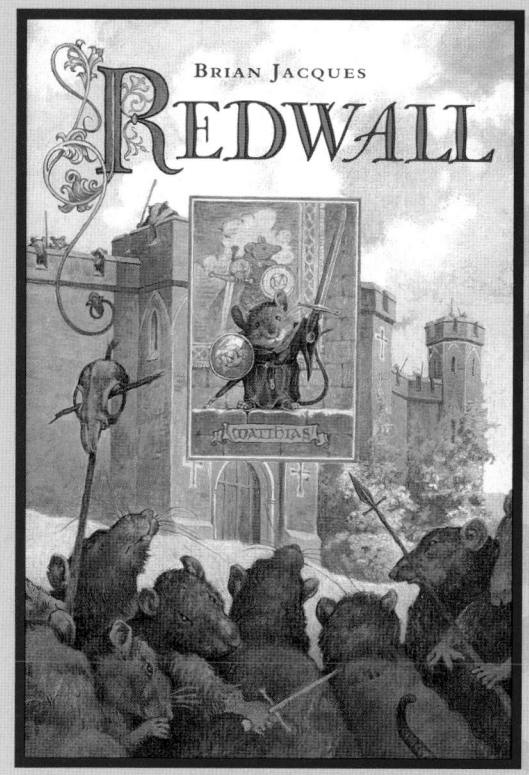

A Selected Bibliography of Jacques's Work

Triss: A Tale from Redwall (2002)
Castaways of the Flying Dutchman (2001)
A Redwall Winter's Tale (2001)
Taggerung: A Tale from Redwall (2001)
Lord Brocktree: A Tale of Redwall (2000)
The Legend of Luke (1999)
Marlfox (1999)
The Long Patrol: A Tale from Redwall (1997)
Pearls of Lutra (1997)
Outcast of Redwall (1996)
The Great Redwall Feast (1995)
The Bellmaker (1994)
Martin the Warrior (1993)
Salamandastron (1992)
Mariel of Redwall (1991)
Seven Strange & Ghostly Tales (1991)
Mattimeo (1990)
Mossflower (1988)
Redwall (1986)

Brian traveled to faraway places such as New York, San Francisco, and Yokohama, Japan. But he soon tired of the lonely life of a sailor.

Returning home to Liverpool, Jacques worked a variety of jobs and began writing music, poetry, and plays. While working as a truck driver, Jacques regularly delivered milk to the Royal Wavertree School for the Blind. He soon began volunteering his time to read to the students there. As he read, ideas for his own story began to form in his mind. He soon began writing the book that would become *Redwall*.

> *"My ideas come crowding into my mind and then they clamour to be let out. I take my little West Highland terrier for a good long walk . . . and we talk it over, and then I sit down in my garden to write until the tale is done."*

Jacques wrote *Redwall* for the children at the school, keeping his audience in mind. Writing for blind students, his style emerged, so that the students could imagine the action easily in their minds. The story was a huge hit with the children at the school.

Jacques had stayed in touch with his former teacher Alan Durband, who read *Redwall* and showed it to a publisher without telling him. The publisher loved the tale and signed Jacques to a five-book contract for the adventure series featuring the battle between the peaceful mice and the evil rats. Brian dedicated his 1995 book *The Bellmaker* to Durband.

Today, the series has grown to sixteen titles, with more in the works.

Before becoming a full-time author, Brian Jacques worked as a merchant seaman, a railway fireman, a longshoreman, a long-distance truck driver, a bus driver, a boxer, a policeman, a postmaster, and a stand-up comic.

The Redwall books have been translated into several languages, including Dutch and Japanese. An animated television series on public television has brought the tales to an even wider audience.

By combining his childhood love of adventure stories with some real-life adventures of his own, Brian Jacques created a series to fire the imaginations of a new generation of young readers.

> *"Be good mice, don't be dirty rats. Remember, television can't take you places the way books can. So read, read, read. When you write, paint pictures with words."*

WHERE TO FIND OUT MORE ABOUT BRIAN JACQUES

BOOKS

Holtze, Sally Holmes, ed. *Seventh Book of Junior Authors & Illustrators.* New York: H. W. Wilson Company, 1996.

WEB SITES

KIDSREADS.COM
http://www.kidsreads.com/authors/au-jacques-brian.asp
To read a biographical sketch of Brian Jacques, a booklist, and transcripts of interviews with the author

REDWALL ABBEY: THE OFFICIAL REDWALL WEB SITE
http://www.redwall.org/
For a biographical sketch of Brian Jacques, book information, descriptions of the Redwall characters, and transcripts of interviews with the author

SCHOLASTIC AUTHORS ONLINE
http://www2.scholastic.com/teachers/authorsandbooks/authorstudies/ authorhome.jhtml?authorID=46&collateralID=5192&displayName=Biography
To read a biographical sketch of Brian Jacques, a booklist, and an interview transcript

BRIAN JACQUES HOSTS A RADIO PROGRAM ON BBC RADIO MERSEYSIDE ON SUNDAY AFTERNOONS IN LIVERPOOL. ON HIS SHOW, BRAIN PERFORMS COMEDY AND PLAYS HIS FAVORITE MUSIC—MOSTLY OPERA. HE IS AN EXPERT ABOUT THE SUBJECT.

Angela Johnson

Born: June 18, 1961

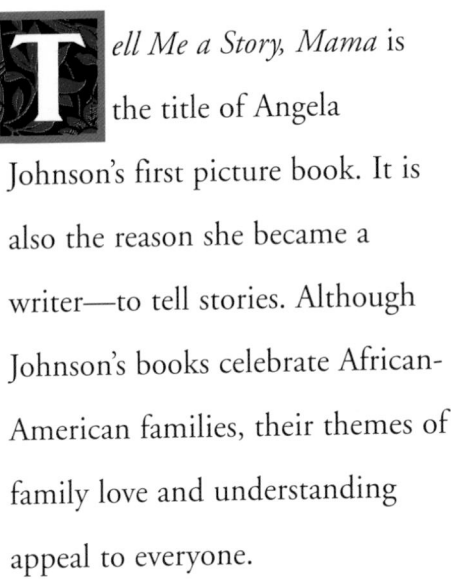

Tell Me a Story, Mama is the title of Angela Johnson's first picture book. It is also the reason she became a writer—to tell stories. Although Johnson's books celebrate African-American families, their themes of family love and understanding appeal to everyone.

Family has always been important to Angela Johnson. She comes from a close-knit family and a long line of storytellers. She was born on June 18, 1961, in Tuskegee, Alabama, to Arthur Johnson, an autoworker, and Truzetta (Hall) Johnson, an accountant. As soon as Angela could talk, she began telling stories. Her parents say that, when she was an

---

JOHNSON HAS KEPT A DIARY OF HER EXPERIENCES
AND DREAMS SINCE SHE WAS EIGHT YEARS OLD.

infant, she would lie awake in her crib telling stories to herself. As she got older, she never tired of listening to the stories her father and grand-father told. In time, storytelling became second nature to her.

Angela grew up in the small town of Shorter, Alabama, and attend-ed Maple Grove School. When her family moved to Windham, Ohio, Angela attended Windham High School. There, she became interested in literature and poetry and began writing down her thoughts and feelings in a diary.

After graduating from high school in 1979, Johnson enrolled at Kent State University in Kent, Ohio. Thinking that she might like to become a teacher or social worker, Johnson chose to study education. But

> *"There is such a rich storytelling tradition in the African-American culture. It's art, dance, and music all rolled into one. I am lucky to be part of this proud tradition."*

before completing her degree, she left Kent State to become a writer. For the next eight years, she worked at a variety of jobs to support herself. She was a child development worker with VISTA (Volunteers in Service to America) and a nanny.

In 1989, Johnson published her first book, *Tell Me a Story, Mama*. It is based on her relationship with her father and the stories he shared with her when she was a child. The success of this book enabled Johnson

IN 1999, JOHNSON RECEIVED A CORETTA SCOTT KING AWARD FOR HER BOOK *HEAVEN*. THE SAME YEAR, HER BOOK *THE OTHER SIDE: SHORTER POEMS* WAS HONORED AS A RUNNER-UP.

A Selected Bibliography of Johnson's Work

Just Like Josh Gibson (2003)

Looking for Red (2002)

Running Back to Ludie (2001)

Down the Winding Road (2000)

When Mules Flew on Magnolia Street (2000)

Maniac Monkeys on Magnolia Street (1999)

Gone from Home: Short Takes (1998)

Heaven (1998)

The Other Side: Shorter Poems (1998)

Songs of Faith (1998)

Daddy Calls Me Man (1997)

The Rolling Store (1997)

The Aunt in Our House (1996)

Humming Whispers (1995)

Shoes Like Miss Alice's (1995)

Joshua by the Sea (1994)

Joshua's Night Whispers (1994)

Mama Bird, Baby Birds (1994)

Toning the Sweep (1993)

Julius (1993)

The Leaving Morning (1992)

One of Three (1991)

Do Like Kyla (1990)

When I Am Old with You (1990)

Tell Me a Story, Mama (1989)

Johnson's Major Literary Awards

2004 Coretta Scott King Author Award
   The First Part Last

2004 Michael L. Printz Award
   The First Part Last

1999 Coretta Scott King Author Award
   Heaven

1999 Coretta Scott King Author Honor Book
   The Other Side: Shorter Poems

1994 Coretta Scott King Author Award
   Toning the Sweep

1991 Coretta Scott King Author Honor Book
   When I Am Old with You

to quit her jobs and write full time. During the early 1990s, she published many books for young children about family life. Her book *Do Like Kyla* is about the love that two sisters share. *When I Am Old with You* is a story about a boy who dreams about growing old with his grandfather. And in the book *One of Three,* a girl shares the joys and frustrations of being the youngest of three sisters in a family.

> *Family storytelling has been the overriding influence in my writing. While my book characters aren't actual living beings, they are part of wholes—my family, living and dead."*

After writing many successful picture books, Angela Johnson published her first novel for young adults in 1993. The novel, called *Toning the Sweep,* celebrates family and friendship. Following the publication of this book, Johnson became even better known as a writer of novels, short stories, and poetry for preteens and teenagers.

Angela Johnson still lives in Ohio, close to her family. She continues to write books for children. Her board books and picture books delight preschoolers and early readers. Her novels, short stories, and poetry books help young adults get through difficult times. Angela Johnson is a gifted storyteller. Her tales capture the hearts of everyone.

WHERE TO FIND OUT MORE ABOUT ANGELA JOHNSON

BOOKS

Holtze, Sally Holmes, ed. *Seventh Book of Junior Authors & Illustrators.* New York: H. W. Wilson Company, 1996.

WEB SITES

AFRICAN AMERICAN LITERATURE BOOK CLUB
http://aalbc.com/authors/angela.htm
To read a biographical account of Angela Johnson and synopses of some of her books

HOUGHTON MIFFLIN: MEET THE AUTHOR
http://www.eduplace.com/kids/hmr/mtai/johnson.html
To read a biographical sketch of and booklist for Angela Johnson

ONE OF ANGELA'S FAVORITE ACTIVITIES IN GRADE SCHOOL WAS TO GO TO THE LOCAL DRUGSTORE TWICE A WEEK TO BUY SNICKERS BARS AND ARCHIE COMIC BOOKS.

Ann Jonas

Born: January 28, 1932

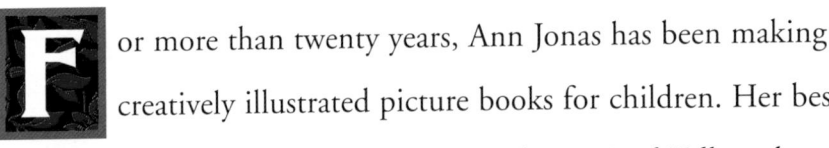

For more than twenty years, Ann Jonas has been making creatively illustrated picture books for children. Her best-known books include *The Quilt; Round Trip; Bird Talk;* and *Aardvarks, Disembark!*

Ann Jonas was born on January 28, 1932, in Flushing, New York. She was taught to think creatively at an early age, since her parents preferred making their own clothes and furniture to buying them in a store. When not helping her parents, Ann and her brother spent many hours playing outdoors. They walked through the fields and parks. They loved to discover new things and use their imaginations. Today, imagination plays a big part in Jonas's books. In one story, she writes about a little girl who thinks gorillas are disguised as bushes and that chimneys look like giraffes.

In Ann's family, drawing was something you did while you were planning a project, not something you did just for its own sake. But

---

JONAS HAS TWO DAUGHTERS, NINA AND AMY.

Ann loved to draw and decided that she wanted to be an artist when she grew up.

After she finished high school, Jonas did not think about going to college. She got a job working in the advertising department of a department store. But she decided that she needed to know much more about art, so she went to art school. She met her husband while studying there. After she finished school, she got a job in a graphic design studio.

In the early 1960s, her husband was drafted into the army. They moved to Germany for several years. Jonas worked

> *"It is wonderful to get feedback from children."*

A Selected Bibliography of Jonas's Work

Bird Talk (1999)
Watch William Walk (1997)
Splash! (1995)
The 13th Clue (1992)
Aardvarks, Disembark! (1990)
Color Dance (1989)
Reflections (1987)
Now We Can Go (1986)
Where Can It Be? (1986)
The Trek (1985)
Holes and Peeks (1984)
The Quilt (1984)
Round Trip (1983)
Two Bear Cubs (1982)
When You Were a Baby (1982)

Jonas's Major Literary Awards

1991 *Boston Globe–Horn Book* Picture Book Honor Book
 Aardvarks, Disembark!

1986 *Boston Globe–Horn Book* Picture Book Honor Book
 The Trek

for an advertising agency while living in Germany. When they returned to the United States, Jonas and her husband opened their own graphic design studio.

Jonas's husband began writing and illustrating books for children. He encouraged Jonas to try to write a children's book. He introduced her to a publisher, who also urged her to write a book. Her first book, *When You Were a Baby,* was published in 1982. The book was successful, and Jonas decided to become a full-time children's book writer and illustrator.

Jonas uses many different styles of illustration for her books and tries to come up with creative ways of making the books interesting for children. Her book *Round Trip* describes a trip from the country to the city. At the end of the book, it can be turned upside down and read backward. When the book is turned over, the story describes the trip back to the country. It took Jonas a long time to get this book just right. *Color Dance* also uses an imaginative technique to get readers' attention. As three dancers wave multicolored scarves

> *"I find that I approach each book quite differently. Each idea seems to need a specific technique and style to most clearly illustrate the point I'm trying to make."*

JONAS'S BOOK *THE QUILT* WAS WRITTEN FOR HER DAUGHTER, NINA. IT IS BASED ON A QUILT THAT JONAS MADE FOR HER.

through the air, children get to learn about different color combinations.

Jonas continues to write and illustrate picture books for children. She lives in New York with her family.

❧

WHERE TO FIND OUT MORE ABOUT ANN JONAS

BOOKS
McElmeel, Sharron L. *100 Most Popular Picture Book Authors & Illustrators.*
Englewood, Colo.: Libraries Unlimited, 2000.

Holtze, Sally Holmes, ed. *Seventh Book of Junior Authors & Illustrators.*
H. W. Wilson Company: New York, 1996.

WEB SITE
NATIONAL CENTER FOR CHILDREN'S ILLUSTRATED LITERATURE
http://www.nccil.org/jonas.html
To read a biography of Ann Jonas

———

WHEN WRITING THE BOOK *AARDVARKS, DISEMBARK!*, JONAS LEARNED
ABOUT THE NUMBER OF ANIMALS THAT ARE NOW EXTINCT OR ENDANGERED.
SHE USED THE BOOK AS A WAY TO TEACH CHILDREN ABOUT PROTECTING THEM.

William Joyce

Born: December 11, 1957

In William Joyce's books, anything can happen. Dinosaurs dance the hokey-pokey. Gorillas wear ties and walk down the street. Uncles ride in flying saucers. How does Joyce explain such bizarre happenings? He says he is simply fighting for "the cause of global silliness."

William Joyce was born on December 11, 1957, in Shreveport, Louisiana. From an early age, he showed a talent for drawing. Art was his favorite subject in school. He spent much of his time as a boy drawing sketches. He started drawing dogs and cats, but before long he was drawing

---

JOYCE WAS ONE OF SEVERAL ILLUSTRATORS WHO WORKED ON THE MOVIE *TOY STORY.*

dinosaurs and spaceships. When William wasn't drawing, he was reading and watching movies and television. This helped shape his artistic imagination. He decided to study filmmaking at Southern Methodist University. But he hoped one day to write and illustrate his own books.

Even before Joyce graduated from college, he began seeking work as an illustrator. He sent samples of his work to publishers. He succeeded in landing a number of assignments to illustrate books by other authors. Joyce was not satisfied, though. He wanted to illustrate his own stories.

He finally got his chance when *George Shrinks* was published in 1985. The book tells the story of a boy who wakes up to find that he has shrunk overnight. Three-inch-tall George finds

> *"My characters are willing to fight for the right to act odd and suave."*

himself in the middle of new adventures because of his size. He dives into a goldfish bowl to feed his pet fish. He saddles his baby brother and rides on his back. *George Shrinks* won a Best Book Award from the *School Library Journal*.

Joyce's next book was *Dinosaur Bob and His Adventures with the Family Lazardo*. In the book, the Lazardos adopt Bob the Dinosaur after they meet him on their annual safari. Bob moves into the family's

---

JOYCE HAS CREATED ILLUSTRATIONS FOR *THE NEW YORKER* AND OTHER MAGAZINES.

A Selected Bibliography of Joyce's Work

Big Time Olie (2002)
Sleepy Time Olie (2001)
Snowie Rolie (2000)
Baseball Bob (1999)
Rolie Polie Olie (1999)
Life with Bob (1998)
Buddy (1997)
The World of William Joyce Scrapbook (1997)
The Leaf Men and the Brave Good Bugs (1996)
Santa Calls (1993)
Bently & Egg (1992)
A Day with Wilbur Robinson (1990)
Dinosaur Bob and His Adventures with the Family Lazardo (1988)
George Shrinks (1985)

home in the suburbs, and soon displays a talent for baseball. The book was very successful, and Bob became one of Joyce's most popular creations. Joyce has written two more books about Bob: *Life with Bob* and *Baseball Bob.*

Joyce created an unusual cast of characters for his next book. In *A Day with Wilbur Robinson,* frogs ride on dogs, goldfish are giants, and lovable uncles keep flying saucers parked behind the house. *A Day with Wilbur Robinson* won a Parents' Choice Award for 1991. Joyce followed that with *Bently & Egg.* Bentley is a frog who tries to help his friend Kack Kack the Duck by egg-sitting. In 1993, Joyce

published *Santa Calls,* about a brother and sister called to the North
Pole by Santa Claus.

Joyce depends on his family for inspira-
tion for his stories. Sometimes Joyce's wife,
Elizabeth, will pose for him when he is trying
to draw a new character. One of Joyce's stories
had its beginnings in a bedtime story he told his daughter, Mary
Katherine. That story became *The Leaf Men and the Brave Good Bugs.*
It tells the story of the battle between the Leaf Men and the evil Spider
Queen to save an elderly woman's rose garden.

> *"My dad says I was born with a pencil in my hand. I always loved drawing."*

WHERE TO FIND OUT MORE ABOUT WILLIAM JOYCE

BOOKS

Holtze, Sally Holmes, ed. *Sixth Book of Junior Authors & Illustrators.*
New York: H. W. Wilson Company, 1989.

WEB SITES

THE BOOK PAGE
http://www.bookpage.com/9610bp/childrens/theleafmen.html
For an interview with William Joyce and information on
The Leaf Men and the Brave Good Bugs

HARPERCHILDRENS.COM
http://www.harperchildrens.com/hch/author/author/joyce/
To read a biographical sketch of William Joyce and synopses of his books

JOYCE'S BOOK *ROLIE POLIE OLIE* IS BASED ON A TELEVISION
PROGRAM THAT JOYCE PRODUCED.

Ezra Jack Keats

Born: March 11, 1916
Died: May 6, 1983

 zra Jack Keats was one of the first American children's authors to use an African-American child as the key character in a book. Keats's award-winning book *The Snowy Day* features a young black boy named Peter. Keats also used Peter in other books. Along with illustrating numerous books for other authors, Keats wrote many of his own books including *Whistle for Willie, A Letter to Amy,* and *Goggles.*

Ezra Jack Keats was born on March 11, 1916, in Brooklyn, New York. At an early age, Keats was interested in being an artist. His mother encouraged him to work on his drawings. She appreciated her son's talent as an artist. Keats's father had a different idea.

He told his son that he could not be successful as an artist. He wanted his son to learn how to do something so he could earn a living.

KEATS'S PARENTS WERE BORN IN POLAND AND DID NOT MEET UNTIL THEY CAME TO AMERICA. A MATCHMAKER ARRANGED THEIR WEDDING.

Keats finally convinced his father that he could make money being an artist when he was paid twenty-five cents to paint a sign for a candy store. His father was pleased and was sure he could earn a living as a sign painter.

When Keats graduated from high school, he was awarded a medal for his art. He was unable to share the medal with his father. Keats's father had died the day before. Keats also received scholarships to attend art schools. He was unable to accept the scholarships because he needed to get a job to support his family.

In 1937, Keats got a job as a mural painter and took art classes at night. Three years

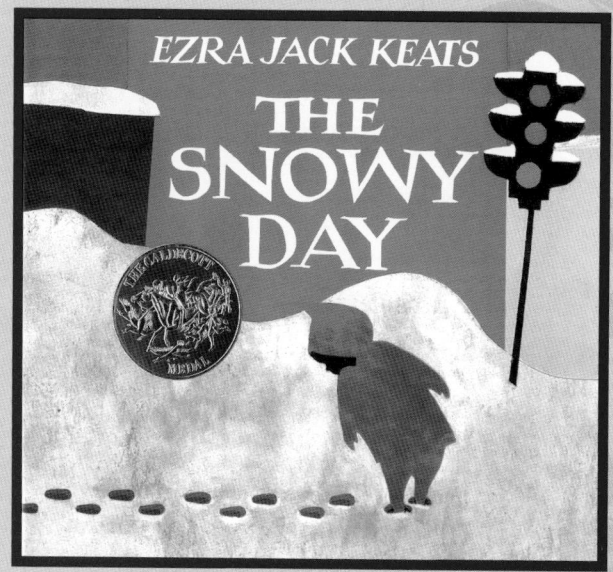

A Selected Bibliography of Keats's Work

One Red Sun: A Counting Book (1999)
Song of the River (Illustrations only, 1993)
Clementina's Cactus (1982)
Louie's Search (1980)
Pet Show! (1972)
Apt. 3 (1971)
Over in the Meadow (1971)
Hi, Cat! (1970)
Goggles (1969)
A Letter to Amy (1968)
John Henry, an American Legend (1965)
Whistle for Willie (1964)
The Snowy Day (1962)
My Dog Is Lost! (1960)
Jubilant for Sure (Illustrations only, 1954)

Keats's Major Literary Awards

1970 *Boston Globe–Horn Book* Picture Book Honor Book
 Hi, Cat!

1970 Caldecott Honor Book
 Goggles

1963 Caldecott Medal
 The Snowy Day

> *"Then began an experience that turned my life around—working on a book with a black kid as hero. None of the manuscripts I'd been illustrating featured any black kids. . . . My book would have him there simply because he should have been there all along."*

later, he became an illustrator for a company that published comic books. In 1943, he joined the army and used his skills as an artist to design camouflage patterns.

After Keats left the army, he went to Paris, France, to study art and to work on his paintings. Many of his paintings would later be displayed in New York art galleries. When he returned to New York, he decided to pursue a career as an illustrator. He painted covers and illustrations for several magazines. He also sold some of his paintings.

In 1954, Keats illustrated *Jubilant for Sure,* a children's book written by Elisabeth Hubbard Lansing. He continued to illustrate many other children's books for other authors. Keats's first book, *My Dog Is Lost!,* was cowritten with Pat Scherr and was published in 1960.

Keats used a special art technique to illustrate his books. He used collages and

> *"I didn't even ask to get into children's books."*

KEATS'S FAMILY HAD MANY TALENTED ARTISTS. HIS BROTHER BECAME A PORTRAIT PHOTOGRAPHER, AND HIS SISTER BECAME A SCULPTOR.

gouache. Gouache is an opaque watercolor paint mixed with a gum that produces a glaze on the pictures. This technique makes Keats's illustrations very different from those in other books.

Keats wrote and illustrated twenty-three children's books. He never married or had any children of his own. He died in New York on May 6, 1983.

❧

WHERE TO FIND OUT MORE ABOUT EZRA JACK KEATS

BOOKS

Kovacs, Deborah, and James Preller. *Meet the Authors and Illustrators: 60 Creators of Favorite Children's Books Talk about Their Work.* Vol. 1. New York: Scholastic, 1991.

Silvey, Anita, ed. *Children's Books and Their Creators.*
Boston: Houghton Mifflin, 1995.

WEB SITES

EDUCATIONAL PAPERBACK ASSOCIATION
http://edupaperback.org/showauth.cfm?authid=32
To read a biographical sketch and booklist for Ezra Jack Keats

UNIVERSITY OF SOUTHERN MISSISSIPPI DE GRUMMOND COLLECTION
http://www.lib.usm.edu/~degrum/keats/main.html
To read a biographical sketch of Ezra Jack Keats, a booklist, and
a description of the making of an Ezra Jack Keats picture book

———

KEATS WAS JEWISH, AND HIS NAME AT BIRTH WAS JACOB KATZ. AFTER WORLD WAR II (1939–1945), HE LEGALLY CHANGED HIS NAME TO EZRA JACK KEATS BECAUSE HE WAS CONCERNED HOW HE WOULD BE TREATED IF PEOPLE KNEW HE WAS JEWISH.

Steven Kellogg

Born: October 26, 1941

Steven Kellogg's job lets him do something he loves—make up stories and draw pictures. Steven has loved to draw since he was a boy. He drew the things he saw around him. He drew the things he saw in books. He drew for his grandma, who was his best friend. He made up stories for his younger sisters. While telling them the stories, he drew pictures at the same time. His sisters called this "telling stories on paper."

Steven was born on October 26, 1941, in Norwalk, Connecticut. As a child, he enjoyed picture books. Animal stories were his favorite. After graduating from high school, Kellogg went to the Rhode

KELLOGG BELIEVES IT IS VERY IMPORTANT FOR ADULTS AND CHILDREN TO SHARE PICTURE BOOKS TOGETHER.

Island School of Design in Providence. He decided to concentrate on studying the art of illustration. Illustration is drawing pictures, usually to go along with a story. During his last year at the Rhode Island School of Design, he was able to live and study in Florence, Italy. That year was very important to him. His experiences in Italy have left him with many memories. He uses these memories as he writes and illustrates his books.

> *"I want the time that the reader shares with me and my work to be an enjoyable experience—one that will encourage a lifetime association with pictures, words, and books."*

Kellogg started his publishing career by illustrating books that were written by other people. In 1967, his first book of illustrations was published. It was called *Gwot! Horribly Funny Hairticklers.* Although he was good at illustrating stories written by other people, he was also interested in writing the stories himself. His first story, *The Wicked Kings of Bloon,* was published in 1970. Since then, Kellogg has had more than 100 books published.

The ideas for Kellogg's books come from many places. One famous character in Kellogg's books is Pinkerton the dog. Pinkerton is not a pretend character. He is Kellogg's real-life dog. Kellogg wrote

ROSE, THE CAT IN *A ROSE FOR PINKERTON,* WAS REALLY KELLOGG'S OLD GROUCHY CAT!

A Selected Bibliography of Kellogg's Work

Clorinda (2002)

A Penguin Pup for Pinkerton (2001)

The Missing Mitten Mystery (2000)

Three Sillies (1999)

A-Hunting We Will Go! (1998)

The Three Little Pigs (1997)

Frogs Jump: A Counting Book (1996)

Snuffles and Snouts (1995)

Parents in the Pigpen, Pigs in the Tub (1993)

Johnny Appleseed: A Tall Tale (1988)

Pecos Bill: A Tall Tale (1986)

How Much Is a Million? (1985)

Paul Bunyan: A Tall Tale (1984)

A Rose for Pinkerton (1981)

The Day Jimmy's Boa Ate the Wash (1980)

Pinkerton, Behave! (1979)

The Mysterious Tadpole (1977)

The Boy Who Was Followed Home (1975)

The Wicked Kings of Bloon (1970)

Gwot! Horribly Funny Hairticklers (Illustrations only, 1967)

Kellogg's Major Literary Awards

1985 *Boston Globe–Horn Book* Picture Book Honor Book
    How Much Is a Million?

these books with the ideas he got from living with Pinkerton.

People enjoy Kellogg's stories and illustrations for several reasons. Kellogg uses humor in his writing and in the illustrations. The illustrations are also colorful and usually fill the entire page. The characters are drawn in a way that gives them movement and life.

Kellogg puts a lot of work into making sure that his pictures add to the words of the

"The pictures are compelling and important and they offer kids an opportunity to journey into themselves and provide an avenue for escape."

story. The pictures actually become part of the story. He sees the
pictures and words like different musical instruments playing together
to produce something wonderful.

అ

WHERE TO FIND OUT MORE
ABOUT STEVEN KELLOGG

BOOKS

Collier, Laurie, and Joyce Nakamura, eds. *Major Authors and Illustrators for
Children and Young Adults.* Detroit: Gale Research, 1993.

Kovacs, Deborah, and James Preller. *Meet the Authors and Illustrators: 60 Creators of Favorite
Children's Books Talk about Their Work.* Vol. 1. New York: Scholastic, 1991.

Norby, Shirley. *Famous Children's Authors.*
Minneapolis: TS Denison & Company, 1988.

WEB SITES

EDUCATIONAL PAPERBACK ASSOCIATION
http://edupaperback.org/showauth.cfm?authid=143
To read an autobiographical sketch and booklist for Steven Kellogg

STEVEN KELLOGG'S OFFICIAL WEB PAGE
http://www.stevenkellogg.com
To read more about Steven Kellogg, to see a gallery of his book covers, and
to find out how to contact him

KELLOGG HAS BEEN AN ETCHING INSTRUCTOR AT AMERICAN
UNIVERSITY AND HAS TAUGHT PRINTMAKING AND PAINTING.

M. E. Kerr

Born: May 27, 1927

As a writer, M. E. Kerr uses many different names. Her real name is Marijane Meaker. She uses the name M. E. Kerr when she writes novels for young adults. She has also written using the names M. J. Meaker, Mary James, Ann Aldrich, and Vin Packer. Kerr's most popular books include *The Son of Someone Famous, Little Little, What I Really Think of You,* and *Night Kites.*

M. E. Kerr was born on May 27, 1927, in Auburn, New York. Her father loved to read and write and had many books in the house. Kerr shared her father's love of writing. She loved to read and was encouraged by her teachers and librarians. Kerr knew at a young age that she wanted to be a writer.

AFTER COLLEGE, KERR SENT STORIES TO MAGAZINES, BUT SHE RECEIVED MANY REJECTION LETTERS. ONE YEAR FOR A HALLOWEEN PARTY, SHE COVERED HERSELF WITH THE LETTERS SHE HAD RECEIVED AND WENT AS A REJECTION NOTICE.

She was not a very good student in school. She was always getting in trouble. Kerr's parents became frustrated with her. They wanted her to be a better student. When she was a teenager, Kerr was sent to a boarding school in Virginia. During the summers, she wrote many stories. She sent them to magazines, but none of the stories was published. Attending a new school did not help Kerr's behavior. She continued to get into trouble. Even though she was suspended during her senior year, Kerr graduated from the school.

Kerr attended a junior college for a short time. She worked on the newspaper at the college. In 1946, she transferred

A Selected Bibliography of Kerr's Work

Books of Fell (2001)
Slap Your Sides (2001)
What Became of Her (2000)
Blood on the Forehead: What I Know about Writing (1998)
"Hello," I Lied (1997)
Deliver Us from Evie (1994)
Linger (1993)
Fell Back (1989)
Night Kites (1986)
What I Really Think of You (1982)
Little Little (1981)
Gentle Hands (1978)
The Son of Someone Famous (1974)
Dinky Hocker Shoots Smack (1972)

"When I write for young adults I know they're still wrestling with . . . problems like winning and losing, not feeling accepted or accepting, prejudice, love. . . . I know my audience hasn't yet made up their minds about everything. . . . Give me that kind of audience any day!"

to the University of Missouri. She started as a journalism student but soon switched to studying English. She wanted to be a fiction writer. When she finished college, she moved to New York and got a job with a publishing company.

Kerr continued to write stories and send them to publishers. Finally, in 1951, she got her first story published in a magazine. This was the start of Kerr's writing career. She wrote several novels and nonfiction books for adults during the next several years.

One of her books included a main character who was a teenager. Kerr's friends encouraged her to write a novel for young adults. She decided to use the name M. E. Kerr for this novel. The book, *Dinky Hocker Shoots Smack,* was published in 1972. Since then, she has published many novels for young adults.

"When I think of myself and what I would have liked to have found in books those many years ago, I remember being depressed by all the neatly tied-up, happy-ending stories, the abundance of winners, the themes of winning, solving, finding—when around me it didn't seem that easy."

KERR'S NOVELS APPEAL TO BOTH BOYS AND GIRLS. SHE USUALLY WRITES FROM THE MALE VIEWPOINT BECAUSE SHE HAS FOUND THAT BOYS WILL NOT READ A BOOK WITH A FEMALE MAIN CHARACTER.

Kerr's novels are about real issues that kids experience. She uses humor in her books. She also writes about serious issues. Her books have dealt with such issues as mental illness, sexuality, drug addiction, and racism. She gets many of the ideas for her books from her own memories of being young.

Kerr continues to write for young adults and others. She lives in East Hampton, New York.

❧

WHERE TO FIND OUT MORE ABOUT M. E. KERR

BOOKS

Kerr, M. E. *Blood on the Forehead: What I Know about Writing.*
New York: HarperCollins, 1998.

Kerr, M. E. *Me, Me, Me, Me, Me: Not a Novel.*
New York: Harper & Row, 1983.

Sutherland, Zena. *Children & Books.*
New York: Addison Wesley Longman, 1997.

WEB SITES

THE M. E. KERR AND MARY JAMES SITE
http://www.mekerr.com/
For a biography of M. E. Kerr, information about her books, and reviews

VANDERGRIFT YOUNG ADULT LITERATURE PAGE
http://scils.rutgers.edu/~kvander/kerr.html
To read a detailed biographical sketch of M. E. Kerr, a booklist,
and a summary of her awards

———

KERR WAS GOOD FRIENDS WITH LOUISE FITZHUGH, THE AUTHOR OF
HARRIET THE SPY. FITZHUGH WAS ONE OF THE PEOPLE WHO
ENCOURAGED KERR TO WRITE NOVELS FOR YOUNG ADULTS.

Eric Kimmel

Born: October 30, 1946

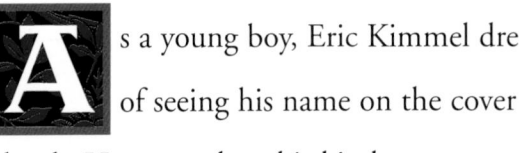

As a young boy, Eric Kimmel dreamed of seeing his name on the cover of a book. He remembers his kindergarten teacher telling the class that one of them could write a book. He was excited by that thought. He decided that he wanted to be a writer even before he knew how to write. Kimmel has been writing books for children and young people for more than twenty-five years. His best-known books include *Sirko and the Wolf: A Ukrainian Tale, Boots and His Brothers: A Norwegian Tale, Anansi and the Talking Melon,* and *Bearhead: A Russian Folktale.*

Eric Kimmel was born on October 30, 1946, in Brooklyn, New York. He loved to read books and write stories as a child. "Somehow, I always knew that I was going to be a writer when I grew up, and that I

BEFORE WRITING A STORY, KIMMEL MAY THINK ABOUT IT FOR SEVERAL YEARS.

would share the stories I loved so much with others," Kimmel says. He especially loved reading books by Dr. Seuss. His favorite was *Horton Hatches the Egg.*

He also loved listening to his grandmother tell him stories. He remembers her telling stories of her childhood in Europe. He loved to hear the folktales she told. "The best present I ever received was a volume of *Grimm's Fairy Tales,* which I loved so much that I literally read it to pieces," Kimmel recalls. The fairy tales and folktales he heard as a boy inspired him to retell these stories in his own books.

> *"When I write a story, I read it aloud over and over again many times, trying to capture the music and rhythm of the words. So you might say that what I'm trying to do is capture in written words the experience of listening to the spoken word."*

When Kimmel finished high school, he attended college to study to become an elementary school teacher. He graduated from college in 1967 and earned a Ph.D. in education in 1973. He worked as a university professor until 1994, when he quit teaching to devote all his time to writing.

Kimmel's first book, *The Tartar's Sword,* was published in 1974. Many of the stories Kimmell retells are stories he heard as child. He

---

KIMMEL'S FIRST BIG SUCCESS WAS HIS BOOK
HERSHEL AND THE HANUKKAH GOBLINS.

A Selected Bibliography of Kimmel's Work

Wonders and Miracles: A Passover Companion (2003)

The Castle of Cats: A Story from Ukraine (2002)

The Jar of Fools: Eight Hanukkah Stories from Chelm (2000)

The Birds' Gift: A Ukrainian Easter Story (1999)

Sirko and the Wolf: A Ukrainian Tale (1997)

Billy Lazroe and the King of the Sea: A Tale of the Northwest (1996)

One Eye, Two Eyes, Three Eyes: A Hutzul Tale (1996)

Anansi and the Talking Melon (1994)

The Gingerbread Man (1993)

Boots and His Brothers: A Norwegian Tale (1992)

Bearhead: A Russian Folktale (1991)

Hershel and the Hanukkah Goblins (1989)

Anansi and the Moss-Covered Rock (1988)

The Tartar's Sword (1974)

also finds material among the large collection of stories and folktales he has collected.

In his books, Kimmel emphasizes the telling of a story. "Stories aren't dead relics, preserved in a jar and put into a glass case for people to gawk at," Kimmel says. "They are alive, and like all living things they grow and change. You are not the same person you were yesterday. You are not the person you will be tomorrow. So it is with stories. They change each time they are told."

> *"I love old things: old books, old pictures, old tools, old songs, and especially old stories."*

Kimmel travels around the country as a storyteller. He is also known as an expert on children's literature. He lives with his family in Oregon where he continues to write books for children and young people.

❧

WHERE TO FIND OUT MORE ABOUT ERIC KIMMEL

BOOKS

McElmeel, Sharron L. *100 Most Popular Picture Book Authors and Illustrators.* Englewood, Colo.: Libraries Unlimited, 2000.

WEB SITES

PENGUIN PUTNAM BIOGRAPHY
http://us.penguingroup.com/nf/Author/AuthorPage/0,,0_1000007664,00.html
To read a biographical sketch of Eric Kimmel

SCHOLASTIC AUTHORS ONLINE
http://www2.scholastic.com/teachers/authorsandbooks/authorstudies/
authorhome.jhtml?authorID=192&collateralID=5202&displayName=Biography
For a biographical sketch of Eric Kimmel, a booklist, and an interview transcript

---

BESIDES WRITING, KIMMEL ENJOYS BIRD WATCHING, BAKING BREAD, SPINNING, RIDING HORSES, AND PLAYING THE BANJO.

Dick King-Smith

Born: March 27, 1922

Dick King-Smith did not begin his writing career until later in his life. He was fifty-six years old when his first children's book was published. He worked as a farmer, salesman, and teacher before becoming a writer. Since then, he has written more than eighty-five books for children and young people. His best-known books include *Babe: The Gallant Pig, The Invisible Dog, The Mouse Butcher,* and *Dragon Boy.*

Dick King-Smith was born on March 27, 1922, in Gloucestershire, England. As a child, Dick was interested in writing poetry. He had no interest in becoming a children's book author.

King-Smith attended college in the late 1930s. When he finished college,

KING-SMITH'S BOOK *THE SHEEP-PIG* WAS PUBLISHED IN THE UNITED STATES AS *BABE: THE GALLANT PIG.* THE BOOK WAS ADAPTED INTO THE MOTION PICTURE *BABE* IN 1995. THE MOVIE WAS NOMINATED FOR SEVERAL ACADEMY AWARDS.

he joined the British army. He fought in Europe during World War II and was wounded.

After he left the army, King-Smith and his wife moved to a farm near where he was born. King-Smith was a farmer for more than twenty years. He loved farming and loved the animals he raised on his farm. Though he worked hard, it was difficult to earn a living as a farmer. He needed to find another job. He worked for three years for a company that sold coats to firefighters. He also worked in a shoe factory. Then he decided to become a teacher.

King-Smith returned to college to be trained as a teacher. He became an

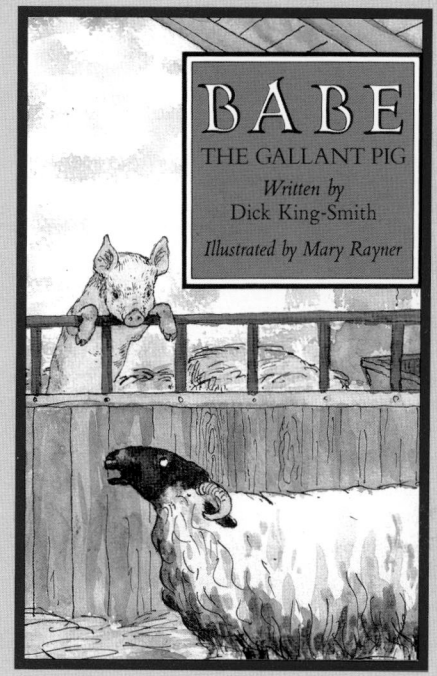

A Selected Bibliography of King-Smith's Work

Funny Frank (2002)

Billy the Bird (2001)

Mysterious Miss Slade (2000)

Spider Sparrow (2000)

Charlie Muffin's Miracle Mouse (1999)

Mr. Ape (1998)

The Water Horse (1998)

Smasher (1997)

A Mouse Called Wolf (1997)

The Stray (1996)

Harriet's Hare (1995)

Dragon Boy (1994)

The Invisible Dog (1993)

The Robber Boy (1991)

Ace, the Very Important Pig (1990)

Martin's Mice (1988)

Harry's Mad (1984)

Babe: The Gallant Pig (1983)

The Mouse Butcher (1982)

The Fox Busters (1978)

King-Smith's Major Literary Awards

1985 *Boston Globe–Horn Book* Fiction Honor Book
Babe: The Gallant Pig

> *"As for trying to fill a need in children's literature, if I am, it is to produce books that can afford adults some pleasure when they read to their children. I write for fun."*

elementary school teacher when he was fifty-three years old. He worked as a teacher for seven years before retiring. While working as a teacher, King-Smith began thinking about writing books for children. His time as a teacher helped him understand what children like to read. His experience as a farmer was also important to him as a writer.

He began using his memories of being a farmer to write his books. He remembered how foxes sometimes came onto his farm and killed the chickens. He decided to write a book in which the chickens work together to chase away the foxes. His first book, *The Fox Busters,* was published in 1978. "I write about animals because I've always kept them, I'm interested in them, I know a bit about them, and I know that children like them," King-Smith notes. "Anyway, it's such fun putting words into their mouths."

> *"If there is a philosophical point behind what I write, I'm not especially conscious of it; maybe I do stress the need for courage, something we all wish we had more of, and I also do feel strongly for underdogs."*

KING-SMITH DOES NOT USE A COMPUTER WHEN HE WRITES. HE WRITES HIS STORIES BY HAND AND THEN TYPES THEM ON HIS OLD TYPEWRITER.

King-Smith has written many children's books. Along with his writing, King-Smith has worked on children's television shows in England. He was involved in the shows *Tumbledown Farm* and *Rub-a-Dub-Tub.* King-Smith currently lives in England near the town where he was born.

WHERE TO FIND OUT MORE ABOUT DICK KING-SMITH

WEB SITES

RANDOM HOUSE: DICK KING-SMITH
http://www.randomhouse.com/kids/dickkingsmith/bio.html
To read a biographical sketch of Dick King-Smith, a booklist, and an interview transcript

YOUNG WRITER
http://www.mystworld.com/youngwriter/authors/dick_kingsmith.html
To read a transcript of an interview with Dick King-Smith

KING-SMITH LIVES WITH HIS WIFE IN A SMALL COTTAGE THAT WAS BUILT IN THE SEVENTEENTH CENTURY. HIS HOUSE IS MORE THAN 300 YEARS OLD.

Norma Klein

Born: May 13, 1938
Died: April 25, 1989

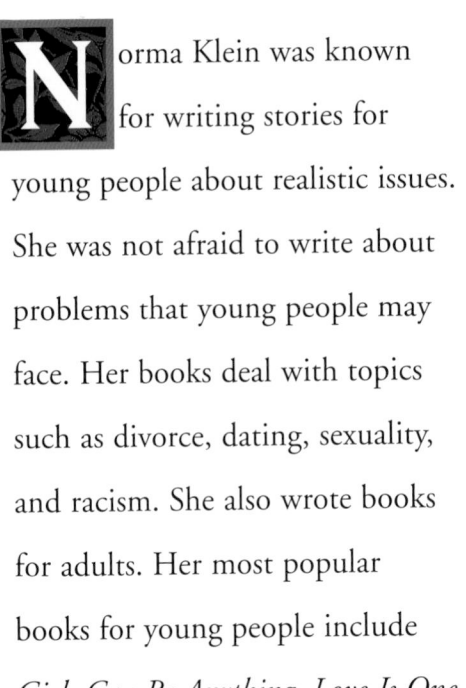 

Norma Klein was known for writing stories for young people about realistic issues. She was not afraid to write about problems that young people may face. Her books deal with topics such as divorce, dating, sexuality, and racism. She also wrote books for adults. Her most popular books for young people include *Girls Can Be Anything, Love Is One of the Choices: A Novel, Sunshine: A Novel,* and *Mom, the Wolf Man, and Me.*

Norma Klein was born on May 13, 1938, in New York City. Growing up in the city, she always thought about being a writer. When

---

KLEIN TAUGHT COURSES IN FICTION AT YALE AND WESLEYAN UNIVERSITIES.

Klein finished high school, she attended Barnard College and Columbia University in New York City.

Klein began her career writing short stories and books for adults. In the 1960s and 1970s, she had many short stories published in literary magazines. She enjoyed writing short stories but found it difficult to get them published. She decided to focus instead on writing novels. In 1972, her first book was published. It included a novella and five of her short stories.

> *"I began writing children's books after reading the millionth picture book to my older daughter and figuring I would like to give it a try."*

After the birth of her first daughter, Klein became interested in writing for young people. She started by writing picture books. Klein then decided to write books for older kids. She thought she would have an easier time publishing these books. Her first book for young people, *Mom, the Wolf Man, and Me,* was also published in 1972. The book was successful and inspired Klein to write other books for older kids.

While other authors write books for either boys or girls, Klein tried to write books that would be interesting for both. She used both boys and girls as main characters in her books. Klein was known for understanding the topics that interest young people. She sometimes wrote

---

Mom, the Wolf Man, and Me was made into a film in 1979.

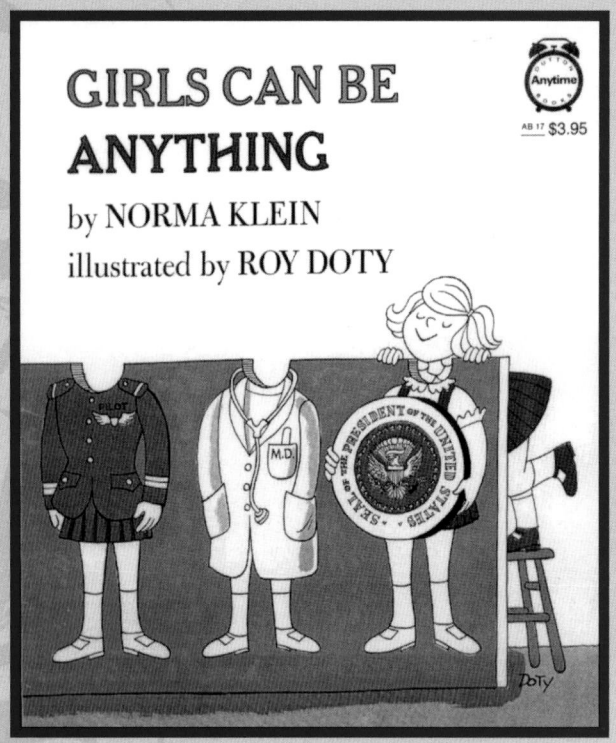

A Selected Bibliography of Klein's Work

Just Friends (1990)

Learning How to Fall (1989)

Going Backwards (1986)

Love Is One of the Choices: A Novel (1978)

Confessions of an Only Child (1974)

Sunshine: A Novel (1974)

Girls Can Be Anything (1973)

Mom, the Wolf Man, and Me (1972)

about issues that are meaningful to kids but upsetting to adults.

Many of Klein's books have been controversial. Several of her books have been targeted by groups wanting them removed from libraries. These groups do not believe the books are appropriate for young people. Klein did not want to cause trouble with her books. She was interested in writing about what kids actually experience. "I'm not a rebel, trying to stir things up just to be

> *"I found I enjoyed writing for children very much, partly perhaps because I got such a warm response to* Mom.*"*

provocative. I'm doing it because I feel like writing about real life," Klein noted.

Klein wrote more than forty books for young people. She also wrote more than sixty short stories for magazines. She published two or three books each year after she became a writer. Klein died on April 25, 1989. She was fifty-one years old.

❧

WHERE TO FIND OUT MORE ABOUT NORMA KLEIN

BOOKS
Something about the Author. Autobiography Series.
Vol. 1. Detroit: Gale Research, 1986.

Sutherland, Zena. *Children and Books.*
New York: Addison Wesley Longman, 1997.

WEB SITE
IN MEMORY OF NORMA KLEIN
http://www.geocities.com/Broadway/1139/normaklein.html
For biographical information on Norma Kein and a list of her books

———

THE PEN/NORMA KLEIN AWARD HONORS KLEIN AND IS GIVEN FOR CHILDREN'S FICTION. IT IS SPONSORED BY KLEIN'S HUSBAND.

Suzy Kline

Born: August 27, 1943

I t's no surprise that Suzy Kline knows what goes in on the classroom. She has been a second- and third-grade teacher for many years. Her classroom experiences have led Suzy to create such memorable children's book characters as Herbie Jones, Horrible Harry, and Mary Marony.

Suzy Weaver was born in Berkeley, California, on August 27, 1943. Her father worked in real estate and her mother was a housewife. After finishing high school, Weaver went to Columbia University in New York City for a year. Then she transferred to the University of California at Berkeley. After

KLINE STARTED WRITING WHEN SHE WAS EIGHT YEARS OLD. HER FIRST WRITING EFFORTS WERE LETTERS TO HER GRANDFATHER, WHO LIVED IN INDIANA. IN THOSE LETTERS, KLINE DESCRIBED WHAT WAS HAPPENING IN HER LIFE.

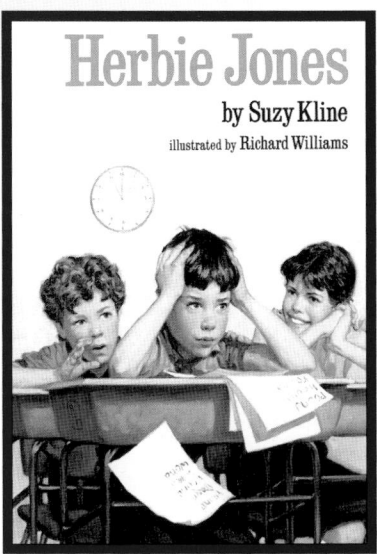

she graduated from Berkeley, she attended California State College in Hayward to get her teaching credentials. Her first job was in an elementary school in Richmond, California.

While she was working in Richmond, Weaver married Rufus O. Kline. Her husband was also a teacher and writer, although he taught college students rather than little kids. The Klines became the parents

A Selected Bibliography of Kline's Work

Horrible Harry and the Dragon War (2002)
Horrible Harry Goes to the Moon (2000)
Marvin and the Meanest Girl (2000)
Molly's in a Mess (1999)
Song Lee and the "I Hate You" Notes (1999)
Horrible Harry Moves Up to Third Grade (1998)
Horrible Harry and the Purple People (1997)
Marvin and the Mean Words (1997)
Horrible Harry and the Dungeon (1996)
Mary Marony and the Chocolate Surprise (1995)
Song Lee and the Leech Man (1995)
Mary Marony, Mummy Girl (1994)
Song Lee and the Hamster Hunt (1994)
Herbie Jones and the Birthday Showdown (1993)
Song Lee in Room 2B (1993)
Herbie Jones and the Dark Attic (1992)
Horrible Harry and the Kickball Wedding (1992)
Orp Goes to the Hoop (1991)
Horrible Harry's Secret (1990)
Orp and the Chop Suey Burgers (1990)
Herbie Jones and Hamburger Head (1989)
Horrible Harry and the Green Slime (1989)
ORP (1989)
Herbie Jones and the Monster Ball (1988)
Ooops! (1988)
Herbie Jones and the Class Gift (1987)
What's the Matter with Herbie Jones? (1986)
Don't Touch (1985)
Herbie Jones (1985)
SHHHH! (1984)

> *"Being a teacher is the most difficult job in the world. At least twice a week I feel like going to an island and not returning to the classroom. But the truth is, I wouldn't do anything else."*

of two daughters, Jennifer and Emily.

In 1976, the Kline family moved to Connecticut. That's where Kline began writing books for children. Her first books were picture books for young children. *SHHHH!* was published in 1984. This book describes a little girl who is told to be quiet by many people during the day. In the end, she finds an acceptable way to be loud. *Don't Touch* was published in 1985. It shows a little boy who is scolded for touching dangerous things until he finds some modeling clay, which he can play with and touch all he wants.

In 1985, Kline published her first book for elementary school students, which introduced a little boy named Herbie Jones to the world of children's books. The books about Herbie show an ordinary little boy and the challenges and delights he faces every day at home and at school. In *What's the Matter with Herbie Jones?,* for example, Herbie must contend with a spelling bee, a school dance, and a girlfriend he doesn't want!

Later, Kline added more "regular kids" to her stories, including a mischievous troublemaker known as Horrible Harry, a little girl who

---

WHEN KLINE VISITS SCHOOLS, SHE ALWAYS BRINGS A BOX OF REJECTION LETTERS AND UNPUBLISHED STORIES. SHE WANTS CHILDREN TO KNOW THAT NOT EVERYTHING SHE WRITES IS GOOD ENOUGH TO BE PUBLISHED.

stutters named Mary Marony, bully Marvin Higgins, shy Song Lee, and Orville Rudemeyer Pygenski Jr., who hates his name and prefers to be called Orp.

> *"Everyday life is full of stories if we just take the time to write them."*

Along with writing about children and teaching them, Kline enjoys visiting schools and talking about her books and characters. For Kline, nothing is more fun than surrounding herself with kids—both real and imaginary!

❧

WHERE TO FIND OUT MORE ABOUT SUZY KLINE

BOOKS

McElmeel, Sharron L. *100 Most Popular Children's Authors.* Englewood, Colo.: Libraries Unlimited, 1999.

WEB SITES

SCHOLASTIC AUTHORS ONLINE

http://www2.scholastic.com/teachers/authorsandbooks/authorstudies/ authorhome.jhtml?authorID=48&collateralID=5204&displayName=Biography

To read an autobiographical sketch by Suzy Kline

SUZY KLINE'S WEB PAGE

http://www.suzykline.com/

For a biographical sketch of Suzy Kline, information about her books, and interactive read-aloud excerpts from some of her works

KLINE HAS WRITTEN AND DIRECTED SCHOOL PLAYS.

E. L. Konigsburg

Born: February 10, 1930

E. L. Konigsburg's books are funny, smart, and different. She has always said that she owes children a good story—and she delivers! She has written more than twenty books in the past thirty years and won just about every award you can name.

E. L. Konigsburg didn't start out to be a writer. She was born on February 10, 1930, in New York City. Her family moved often, and she grew up mostly in small mill towns in Pennsylvania. She read and drew a lot as a child and was an excellent student. No one in her family had ever graduated from college, but that didn't stop her. She earned her bachelor's degree in

WHEN SHE WAS TEACHING CHEMISTRY AT A PRIVATE GIRLS' SCHOOL, E. L. KONIGSBURG REALIZED SHE WAS MORE INTERESTED IN WHAT WAS GOING ON INSIDE HER STUDENTS' HEADS THAN IN THEIR CHEMISTRY EXPERIMENTS.

chemistry, got married, worked in a laboratory, went to graduate school, and taught science at a private girls' school.

Konigsburg had three children—Paul, Laurie, and Ross. She waited until all three were in school before becoming an author. She wrote in the morning while they were at school and read what she had written when they came home for lunch. They were a good audience—and a tough one! And since she had always loved painting, she also illustrated many of her books, using her children as models.

> *"I try to let the telling be like fudge-ripple ice cream. You keep licking the vanilla, but every now and then you come to something darker and deeper and with a stronger flavor."*

Konigsburg has written novels about modern children and novels about historic figures. But all of her books have some things in common. They are sharp and witty and filled with characters you remember. Most of the children in her books are searching for answers to the same basic questions: Who am I, and what makes me me? Am I normal? Am I weird? How am I like everyone else, and how am I different? Do I care if I'm different? Isn't it better to be me?

E. L. Konigsburg writes her books carefully. She usually spends a year to a year and a half on each book—and more if she has to do a lot

A PROUD TASTE FOR SCARLET AND MINIVER AND THE SECOND MRS. GIACONDA MIGHT BE CALLED HISTORICAL FANTASIES. THE FIRST BOOK IS ABOUT THE MEDIEVAL QUEEN ELEANOR OF AQUITAINE, AND THE OTHER FEATURES LEONARDO DA VINCI.

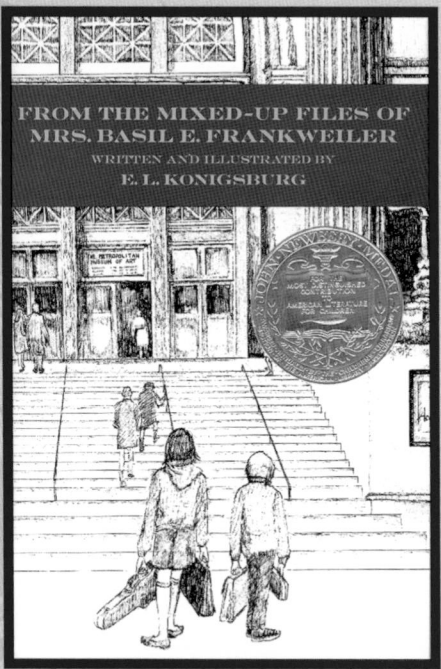

A Selected Bibliography of Konigsburg's Work

Silent to the Bone (2000)
The View from Saturday (1996)
Amy Elizabeth Explores Bloomingdale's (1992)
Samuel Todd's Book of Great Inventions (1991)
Samuel Todd's Book of Great Colors (1989)
Up From Jericho Tel (1986)
Journey to an 800 Number (1982)
Throwing Shadows (1979)
Father's Arcane Daughter (1977)
The Second Mrs. Giaconda (1975)
A Proud Taste for Scarlet and Miniver (1973)
About the B'nai Bagels (1969)
From the Mixed-Up Files of Mrs. Basil E. Frankweiler (1967)
Jennifer, Hecate, Macbeth, William McKinley, and Me, Elizabeth (1967)

Konigsburg's Major Literary Awards

1997 Newbery Medal
  The View from Saturday

1968 Newbery Honor Book
  Jennifer, Hecate, Macbeth, William McKinley, and Me, Elizabeth

1967 Newbery Medal
  From the Mixed-Up Files of Mrs. Basil E. Frankweiler

of research. She writes and revises and erases and rewrites. She is very hard on herself because she thinks that writing for children demands excellence.

Besides her novels, Konigsburg has written and illustrated a number of picture books. Now that her children are all grown up, she sometimes uses her grandchildren as inspira-

"Finish. The difference between being a writer and being a person of talent is the discipline it takes to apply the seat of your pants to the seat of your chair and finish. Don't talk about doing it. Do it. Finish."

tion. She lives on the beach in north Florida, and she loves to read and write and draw and paint. She also loves walking on the beach and going to movies. Whatever she does, she is always on the lookout for new ideas for books.

⁂

WHERE TO FIND OUT MORE ABOUT E. L. KONIGSBURG

BOOKS

Kovacs, Deborah, and James Preller. *Meet the Authors and Illustrators: 60 Creators of Favorite Children's Books Talk about Their Work.* Vol. 1. New York: Scholastic, 1991.

Rockman, Connie C., ed. *Eighth Book of Junior Authors and Illustrators.* New York: H. W. Wilson Company, 2000.

WEB SITES

EDUCATIONAL PAPERBACK ASSOCIATION
http://edupaperback.org/showauth.cfm?authid=251
To read an autobiographical sketch and booklist for E. L. Konigsburg

SCHOLASTIC AUTHORS ONLINE
http://www2.scholastic.com/teachers/authorsandbooks/authorstudies/ authorhome.jhtml?authorID=644&collateralID=5205&displayName=Biography
To read an autobiographical sketch by E. L. Konigsburg,
a booklist, and the transcript of an interview with the author

WHEN A PUBLISHER WANTED TO REVISE A CHAPTER IN *FROM THE MIXED-UP FILES OF MRS. BASIL E. FRANKWEILER* THAT INVOLVED CHILDREN STANDING ON TOILET SEATS IN THE BATHROOM, KONIGSBURG REFUSED.

Kathryn Lasky

Born: June 24, 1944

As a young girl, Kathryn Lasky was not interested in reading. "The truth was that I didn't really like the kind of books they had you reading at school," Lasky says. "So I made a voluntary withdrawal from reading in school." She did

love the stories that her mother read to her at home. She also loved to make up her own stories. This love of storytelling inspired her to become an award-winning author of children's books. Lasky's best-known books for children include *The Night Journey, The Weaver's Gift, Pageant,* and *Double Trouble Squared.*

Kathryn Lasky was born on June 24, 1944, in Indianapolis, Indiana. When she was growing up, she was always thinking

LASKY'S BOOK *SUGARING TIME* WAS MADE INTO A VIDEO IN **1988.**

about stories. Sometimes she wrote down her stories; other times she just thought about stories. Other than the writing she did for school assignments, Kathryn did not share her stories. She did not share her writing with other people until she was much older.

Kathryn had always thought about being a writer, but she thought of writing as more of a hobby than a profession. It was not until she graduated from the University of Michigan that she thought about becoming a professional writer. She first worked as an English teacher. She also did some writing for magazines.

Lasky finally began sharing her writing with other people.

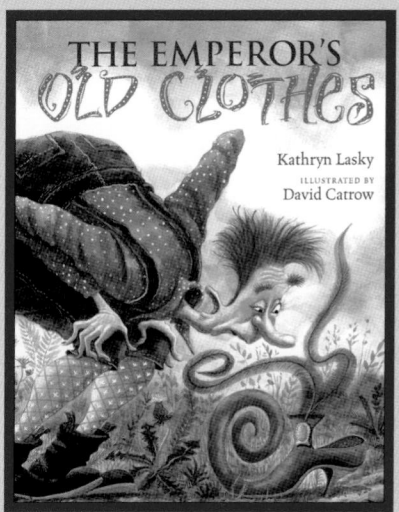

A Selected Bibliography of Lasky's Work

Before I Was Your Mother (2003)
The Man Who Made Time Travel (2002)
Baby Love (2001)
First Painter (2000)
The Emperor's Old Clothes (1999)
Alice Rose & Sam: A Novel (1998)
The Gates of the Wind (1995)
Cloud Eyes (1994)
Think Like an Eagle: At Work with a Wildlife Photographer (1992)
Double Trouble Squared (1991)
Sea Swan (1988)
The Bone Wars (1988)
Pageant (1986)
Puppeteer (1985)
Sugaring Time (1983)
Jem's Island (1982)
The Night Journey (1981)
The Weaver's Gift (1980)
Tall Ships (1978)
Tugboats Never Sleep (1977)
Agatha's Alphabet, with Her Very Own Dictionary (1975)

Lasky's Major Literary Awards

2004 Orbis Pictus Honor Book
  The Man Who Made Time Travel

1984 Newbery Honor Book
  Sugaring Time

1981 *Boston Globe–Horn Book* Nonfiction Award
  The Weaver's Gift

She showed her stories to her parents and her husband. She continued to work on her writing while she worked as a teacher. Her first book, *Agatha's Alphabet, with Her Very Own Dictionary,* was published in 1975. Since that time, Lasky has written many other books, including nonfiction, historical fiction, and picture books.

> *"When I was growing up I was always thinking up stories— whether I wrote them down or not didn't seem to matter. I was a compulsive story maker."*

Most of Lasky's writing has been nonfiction. She does a great deal of research on a topic before she begins writing. She tries to write about things that are interesting to young people. "In my own experience in writing nonfiction, I have always tried hard to listen, smell, and touch the place that I write about," Lasky says. She also writes books about her own experiences.

Lasky enjoys writing many kinds of books for adults and young people. She has found that writing for young people is the most enjoyable. "I feel the same vulnerability that young people feel," Lasky notes. "When I was young, my mother used to tell me, 'People will say this is the best time of your life, but it's not. It's the worst.' Adolescence is a time of pain and anxiety, and stories come out of that tension. I seem to connect with that feeling pretty well."

———

LASKY USES HER MARRIED NAME, KATHRYN LASKY KNIGHT, FOR HER ADULT BOOKS.

Lasky's husband, Christopher Knight, is a photographer and has provided photographs for several of her books. Lasky lives with her husband in Cambridge, Massachusetts. She continues to write for children, young people, and adults.

> *"I really do not care if readers remember a single fact. What I do hope is that they come away with a sense of joy."*

❧

WHERE TO FIND OUT MORE ABOUT KATHRYN LASKY

BOOKS

Kovacs, Deborah, and James Preller. *Meet the Authors and Illustrators: 60 Creators of Favorite Children's Books Talk about Their Work.* Vol. 2. New York: Scholastic, 1991.

Something about the Author. Vol. 112.
Detroit: Gale Research, 2000.

WEB SITE

SCHOLASTIC AUTHORS ONLINE
*http://www2.scholastic.com/teachers/authorsandbooks/authorstudies/
authorhome.jhtml?authorID=51&collateralID=5210&displayName=Biography*
To read a biographical sketch of Kathryn Lasky, a booklist,
and the transcript of an interview with the author

LASKY'S FIRST NONFICTION BOOK WAS *TUGBOATS NEVER SLEEP.*

Patricia Lauber

Born: February 5, 1924

Patricia Lauber has a special gift: She makes science interesting and easy for kids to understand and enjoy. During a career that has spanned nearly five decades, Patricia has penned more than eighty books. She has written about everything from penguins to planets, from the Ice Age to icebergs.

Patricia Lauber was born in New York City on February 5, 1924. As a child, Patricia loved listening to the stories that her mother read aloud to her. Patricia soon realized that, if she learned to read, she could have stories anytime she wanted. After she learned to read and

THE UNIVERSITY OF MINNESOTA HAS A COLLECTION OF
PATRICIA LAUBER'S PAPERS. THEY INCLUDE MANUSCRIPTS, PROOFS,
AND OTHER ITEMS CONNECTED WITH LAUBER'S BOOKS.

write, Patricia began creating her own tales and adventures. Everyone who read Patricia's stories loved them.

After graduating from college in 1945, Lauber knew what she wanted to do: be a writer. She returned to New York City, the capital of the publishing world. Her first job was as a writer for a magazine for grown-ups called *Look.* A year later, Patricia left *Look* to take a job as a writer and editor at *Junior Scholastic,* a newsmagazine for kids.

At Scholastic, Lauber wrote and edited stories for kids. While there, she also published her first book for children. The book, called *Magic Up Your Sleeve,* is nonfiction. In 1956, Lauber became the editor in chief of *Science World.* There, she began to perfect her skills as a science writer.

How does Lauber go about writing her books? First, she chooses a topic that interests her. Although Lauber has no training as a scientist, she is an excellent researcher. She makes sure that she has the most up-to-date information available on her subject. Finally, Lauber finds a way to share what she has learned with readers so they will understand the information and enjoy the book.

> *"Children are born curious, wanting and needing to understand the world around them, wanting to know why, how, and what: the very questions that scientists ask."*

LAUBER MARRIED RUSSELL FROST III IN 1981. THEY LIVE IN CONNECTICUT.

BY PATRICIA LAUBER

A Selected Bibliography of Lauber's Work

The True-or-False Book of Dogs (2003)

What You Never Knew about Tubs, Toilets, & Showers (2001)

Purrfectly Purrfect: Life at the Acatemy (2000)

The Tiger Has a Toothache (1999)

Flood: Wrestling with the Mississippi (1996)

Be a Friend to Trees (1994)

Alligators: A Success Story (1993)

Seeing Earth from Space (1990)

The News about Dinosaurs (1989)

Volcano: The Eruption and Healing of Mount St. Helens (1986)

Seeds Pop, Stick, Glide (1980)

What's Hatching Out of that Egg? (1979)

Everglades Country: A Question of Life or Death (1973)

Your Body and How It Works (1962)

Clarence, the TV Dog (1955)

Lauber's Major Literary Awards

1991 Orbis Pictus Honor Book
   Seeing Earth from Space

1990 Orbus Pictus Honor Book
   The News about Dinosaurs

1987 Newbery Honor Book
   Volcano: The Eruption and Healing of Mount St. Helens

Throughout Lauber's career, a number of her books have been singled out for special awards. Her books have been chosen as New York Academy of Sciences Honor Books as well as Newbery Honor Books. Lauber has also received several awards for her lifetime contributions to children's literature.

What makes Lauber's science books so special? Lauber believes that, like fiction, a good science book has a story line. She makes her story lines interesting and exciting, so that kids will want to know what happens next.

> *"I was born wanting to write."*

Lauber also carefully selects illustrations to accompany and explain her words.

Lauber also writes fiction for kids. Her best-known fiction books are the five Clarence books. The title character is a lovable dog based on Lauber's own dog named Clarence. One day, Lauber told a friend a silly story about her dog. The friend enjoyed the tale, and recommended that Lauber write it down. Lauber did, and the first of the Clarence books, *Clarence, the TV Dog,* was born.

When Lauber isn't researching and writing her next book, she likes to travel. She has been all over the United States and Europe. Lauber's trips sometimes spark new ideas for her writing.

❧

WHERE TO FIND OUT MORE ABOUT PATRICIA LAUBER

BOOKS
Sutherland, Zena. *Children & Books.*
New York: Addison Wesley Longman, 1997.

WEB SITE
HOUGHTON MIFFLIN: MEET THE AUTHOR
http://www.eduplace.com/kids/hmr/mtai/lauber.html
To read a biographical sketch and booklist for Patricia Lauber

LAUBER SAYS THAT MOST OF HER FICTION BOOKS ARE BASED ON DOGS OR HORSES SHE HAS KNOWN.

Robert Lawson

Born: October 4, 1892
Died: May 26, 1957

When Robert Lawson was growing up in Montclair, New Jersey, his family lived in a house that used to belong to famous painter George Innes. Lawson's room was Innes's old studio. Even so, it was a long time before Lawson decided to become an artist.

"I did not, as a child, have any particular interest in drawing and did none until my last year in high school, when it was pointed out to me that I must prepare to do something in the world," he wrote years later.

Robert Lawson was born on October 4, 1892. In the early 1910s, he attended what is now called the Parsons School of Design in New York City. Then he set out to establish himself as an artist, designing ads and stage sets and producing illustrations for newspa-

---

THE STORY OF FERDINAND WAS CONTROVERSIAL WHEN IT WAS PUBLISHED JUST BEFORE THE BEGINNING OF WORLD WAR II (1939–1945). SOME PEOPLE THOUGHT IT WAS A PACIFIST STORY, AGAINST ALL WAR. IN GERMANY, ADOLF HITLER BANNED *FERDINAND*.

pers and magazines. In 1922, Lawson married Marie Abrams, an author and illustrator. The two bought a house in Connecticut, and then spent three years paying for it by designing greeting cards at the rate of one a day. Lawson illustrated his first children's book, *The Wonderful Adventures of Little Prince Toofat* by George Randolph Chester, in 1922. But he was unhappy with the quality of the printed book, so he didn't do any more for quite awhile.

The Lawsons eventually returned to New York. They felt they had lost touch with the publishing world, and it was probably true. When Lawson got his next book to illustrate, he learned that the editor would

A Selected Bibliography of Lawson's Work

Adam of the Road (1970)

The Spring Rider (1968)

The Story of Simpson and Sampson (1968)

The Great Wheel (1957)

The Tough Winter (1954)

Rabbit Hill (1944)

They Were Strong and Good (1940)

Ben and Me: A New and Astonishing Life of Benjamin Franklin as Written by His Good Mouse Amos (1939)

The Sword in the Stone (Illustrations only, 1939)

Mr. Popper's Penguins (Illustrations only, 1938)

Wee Gillis (Illustrations only, 1938)

Four & Twenty Blackbirds (Illustrations only, 1937)

The Story of Ferdinand (Illustrations only, 1936)

Wee Men of Ballywooden (Illustrations only, 1930)

The Wonderful Adventures of Little Prince Toofat (Illustrations only, 1922)

Lawson's Major Literary Awards

1958 Newbery Honor Book
The Great Wheel

1945 Newbery Medal
Rabbit Hill

1941 Caldecott Medal
They Were Strong and Good

1939 Caldecott Honor Book
Wee Gillis

1938 Caldecott Honor Book
Four & Twenty Blackbirds

> *"My mother taught me to like good books. She never forbade my reading trashy books or the funny papers; she didn't care what I read, as long as I was reading something."*

have given it to him earlier, but he thought Lawson was dead.

That book was Arthur Mason's *Wee Men of Ballywooden,* and Lawson's whimsical drawings attracted attention. He was hired to illustrate more of Mason's books and soon was spending most of his time on children's books.

Many of the books Lawson illustrated in the 1930s are forgotten today, but some are still read, such as Richard and Florence Atwater's *Mr. Popper's Penguins* and *The Sword in the Stone* by T. H. White. Perhaps his best-known book was *The Story of Ferdinand,* published in 1936. The story about a bull who would rather smell flowers than fight was written by Lawson's friend Munro Leaf and became a classic.

Lawson soon started writing his own books. The first was *Ben and Me: A New and Astonishing Life of Benjamin Franklin as Written by His Good Mouse Amos,* a look at the life of Benjamin Franklin through the eyes of a mouse. (Lawson eventually wrote more of these history-through-animals books. One was narrated by Paul Revere's horse, another by Christopher Columbus's parrot.) Lawson liked history. His book *They Were Strong and Good* tells the story of his own family. It won the Calde-

---

WHEN MUNRO LEAF FIRST SHOWED ROBERT LAWSON HIS STORY ABOUT FERDINAND THE BULL, LAWSON THOUGHT IT WAS FUNNY, BUT HE DIDN'T WANT TO ILLUSTRATE IT. "I HAD NEVER DRAWN A BULL IN MY LIFE," HE SAID.

cott Medal for illustration. Lawson also wrote stories about the animals that lived near his house. One of them, *Rabbit Hill*, won the Newbery Medal. Lawson was the first writer/artist to win both the Newbery and the Caldecott Medals.

Lawson died in 1957. Nearly fifty years later, his books are still attracting new young readers.

> *"I have never, as far as I can remember, given one moment's thought as to whether any drawing that I was doing was for adults or children. I have never changed one conception or line or detail to suit the supposed age of the readers."*

WHERE TO FIND OUT MORE ABOUT ROBERT LAWSON

BOOKS

McElmeel, Sharron L. *100 Most Popular Children's Authors.*
Englewood, Colo.: Libraries Unlimited, 1999.

Sutherland, Zena. *Children and Books.*
New York: Addison Wesley Longman, 1997.

WEB SITES

BUD PLANET
http://www.bpib.com/illustrat/lawson.htm
To read a biographical sketch of Robert Lawson

THE SCOOP
http://friend.ly.net/users/jorban/biographies/lawsonrobert/index.html
For a biographical sketch and booklist for Robert Lawson

LAWSON'S MOTHER BELIEVED IN GOOD BOOKS. HER
WORD FOR THE OTHER KIND WAS "SCULCH."

Edward Lear

Born: May 12, 1812
Died: January 29, 1888

Edward Lear wrote poetry and created illustrations more than one hundred and fifty years ago. His work is still read by children throughout the world, and many of his poems are being published with new illustrations even today. He wrote many poems, nonsense songs, and stories for children. His best-known book is *The Owl and the Pussycat.*

Edward Lear was born into a wealthy family on May 12, 1812, in London, England. His father was a stockbroker. When Edward was about four years old, his father lost a lot of money from his stocks. The family had to give up their wealthy lifestyle. Edward was sent to live with his sister Ann. She was twenty-

LEAR HAD TWENTY BROTHERS AND SISTERS.

one years older than he was and served as his mother. Edward never knew his real mother well.

Edward was not a healthy child. When he was about five years old, it was discovered that he had epilepsy, a disease of the central nervous system. He suffered from asthma and had poor eyesight. He also experienced severe mood changes. Edward was often depressed as a young boy. His childhood was not happy.

Edward Lear started to make a living as an artist when he was fifteen years old. He drew sketches of the human body and sold them to medical students for their studies. He also made money by teaching other people how to draw.

When Edward Lear was eighteen years old, he illustrated a book about parrots for the city zoo. He was hired by the earl of Derby to create a collection of drawings of rare birds. Working on the collection allowed him to travel to Italy and Greece to sketch birds that he saw.

Lear was also asked to entertain the earl of Derby's grandchildren. He wrote nonsense limericks

> *"There was an Old Man with a beard, who said, 'It is just as I feared!—Two Owls and a Hen, four Larks and a Wren, Have all built their nests in my beard!'"*
> *—from* A Book of Nonsense

IN 1846, LEAR GAVE DRAWING LESSONS TO ENGLAND'S QUEEN VICTORIA!

A Selected Bibliography of Lear's Work

A New Nonsense Alphabet (1988)

Lear in the Original (1975)

The Quangle Wangle's Hat (1969)

The Owl and the Pussycat (1953)

A Nonsense Alphabet (1952)

The Complete Nonsense of Edward Lear (1947)

The Complete Nonsense Book (1912)

Nonsense Songs and Stories (1895)

More Nonsense Pictures, Rhymes, Botany, and Alphabets (1871)

A Book of Nonsense (1846)

Lear's Major Literary Awards

1999 *Boston Globe–Horn Book* Picture Book Honor Book
  The Owl and the Pussycat

and other poems that he shared with the children. In 1846, he added illustrations to the verses and published his first book, *A Book of Nonsense.* He continued to write verse and published several other collections of poems and limericks.

Even though he is best known as a children's author, Lear was a very good painter. He studied at famous art schools and traveled throughout Europe studying art. He created many drawings, oil

"Henceforth, let the inhabitants of the world be divided into two classes—them as has seen the Taj Mahal and them as hasn't."

paintings, and watercolor paintings during his life. There are large collections of his paintings in galleries and museums in England.

After his years of traveling, Edward Lear settled in San Remo, Italy. He died there on January 29, 1888. He was seventy-five years old.

❧

WHERE TO FIND OUT MORE ABOUT EDWARD LEAR

BOOKS

Kamen, Gloria. *Edward Lear, King of Nonsense: A Biography.*
New York: Atheneum Books, 1990.

Lewis, J. Patrick. *Boshblobberbosh: Runcible Poems for Edward Lear.*
New York: Harcourt, Brace, 1998.

WEB SITES

EDWARD LEAR HOME PAGE
http://www.nonsenselit.org/Lear/
For a biographical sketch of Edward Lear, a booklist, and a selection of his art

THE KNITTING CIRCLE
http://www.sbu.ac.uk/~stafflag/edwardlear.html
To read a biographical sketch of and a booklist for Edward Lear

---

LEAR DID NOT USE HIS OWN NAME WHEN HE PUBLISHED HIS FIRST BOOK,
A BOOK OF NONSENSE. INSTEAD, HE USED THE NAME DERRY DOWN DERRY.

INDEX

C